CHILD'S BIBLE

IN COLOUR

The New Testament

First published in Great Britain in 1969
and distributed by Wolfe Publishing Ltd.

First published in the U.S.A. in 1978 by Paulist Press
Editorial Office: 1865 Broadway, New York, N.Y. 10023
Business Office: 545 Island Road, Ramsey, N.J. 07446

Library of Congress
Catalog Card Number: 78-51445
ISBN: 0-8091-2118-2

Printed and Bound in the
United States of America

A CHILD'S BIBLE

IN COLOUR

The New Testament

Re-written for children by
SHIRLEY STEEN

Illustrated by
CHARLES FRONT

PAULIST PRESS
New York, N.Y./Ramsey, N.J./Toronto

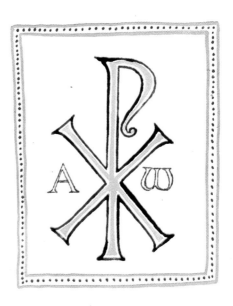

THIS story takes place in Palestine nearly 2,000 years ago. Traditionally the home of the Jews, the entire country was ruled by the Romans who had conquered it many years before. The Jews felt humiliated by this and were awaiting the arrival of the Messiah, one who according to their prophets would be sent by God to lead the Jews against the Romans and restore the Jews to their former glory.

The Jews, who lived mainly in and around Jerusalem where they had their Temple, observed strict religious laws, and looked down on non-Jews. They also despised their fellow Jews who worked for the Romans as tax collectors, and regarded those who did this job as sinners.

Within the Jewish community itself there were various groups which are frequently mentioned in the story. Pharisees, a group of devout Jews, believed in life after death; Saducees, a group of priestly Jews, very rich and very strict, did not believe in life after death. The Chief Priests of the Temple had enormous influence.

Herod the King (mentioned at the beginning of the story) was a Roman-appointed King. After his death a relative of his, also called Herod, was appointed Tetrarch (which meant ruler but not king) of a section of Palestine.

This abridged version of the New Testament is told in simple language for today's child and, by means of the reference given in each page, can be used as a stepping stone to the authorised Bible.

N

W E

S

GREAT SEA

EGYPT

CONTENTS

CHAPTER ONE

ELISABETH AND ZACHARIAS

ST. LUKE 1—1-56

In the days when Herod was king of Judea there was a priest called Zacharias who had a wife, Elisabeth. They had no children and were now very old. One day whilst Zacharias was in the Temple burning incense an angel suddenly appeared before him.

Zacharias was overwhelmed, but the angel said, "I am the angel Gabriel. Do not be afraid Zacharias. Your prayers have been heard and your wife Elisabeth will bear a son. He will be one of God's men. And you must call him John. And from this moment you will be speechless, until your son is born."

I

The congregation waiting outside the Temple were astonished when Zacharias came out, and they could see that he was dumb. They realised that he had seen a vision in the Temple.

Zacharias returned home to his wife. Some weeks later she discovered that she was going to have a baby and she was very happy.

MARY IS CHOSEN

ST. LUKE 1—1-56

Now Elisabeth had a cousin called Mary who lived in the city of Nazareth in the district of Galilee. Mary was engaged to marry a carpenter called Joseph.

One day, a few months before Elisabeth's baby was due to be born, the angel Gabriel came into the room where Mary was, and said, "Greetings, Mary. Do not be frightened. God loves you very much. You are to have a son, and you will call him Jesus. He will be known as the Son of God and he will reign over the people of Jacob for ever."

And Mary replied, "How can it be that I shall have a child. I am not married."

Gabriel reassured her that this was God's will and added, "Your cousin Elisabeth who has always been unable to have children and who is now quite old, has also conceived a son."

Mary, convinced, said, "I accept the Lord's wishes. I belong to the Lord." And the angel departed.

She wasted no time in getting ready and travelled to visit Elisabeth in Jerusalem. They greeted each other and Elisabeth said, "I am honoured that you should visit me, you who are to be the mother of my Lord."

"I am full of praise for God, and joy," said Mary. "Future generations will call me the happiest woman who ever lived." Mary stayed with Elisabeth for three months then returned to her home.

JOSEPH'S DREAM

ST. MATTHEW 1—18-25

When Joseph saw that Mary was pregnant he felt obliged to break off the engagement, but quietly since he did not want her to be publicly disgraced. But whilst he was thinking it over, he had a dream in which an angel of God appeared and told him: "Joseph, Mary has conceived through the Holy Spirit. She will give birth to a son whom you will call Jesus, which means Saviour, for he has been chosen to save the people from their sins. Do not be afraid to marry Mary."

When Joseph awoke he did as the angel had told him.
And soon afterwards he and Mary were married.

THE BIRTH OF JOHN

ST. LUKE 1—59-66

Meanwhile Elisabeth's son was born. When he was eight days old and was to be circumcised, everyone expected that he would be named Zacharias after his father. But his mother said: "He is to be called John." At this everyone was very surprised and made signs to Zacharias, asking what name he wanted. Zacharias beckoned for something on which to write, and he wrote "His name is John".

And immediately his power of speech came back to him, and the first words he spoke were prayers to God. And all the people were astonished by the events and the news was recounted throughout Judea.

THE BIRTH OF JESUS

ST. LUKE 2—1-20

When it was nearly time for Mary's child to be born, a law was announced by Augustus Caesar that all the people in the world should be registered and everybody had to go to the town where they had been born for this registration to take place. Joseph and Mary went from Nazareth to Bethlehem.

Although they looked everywhere for a room to stay, the town was full so they had to sleep in a stable and here Mary's baby was born, and she wrapped him up and laid him in a manger.

Not far away there were some shepherds looking after their flocks of sheep throughout the night. And suddenly an angel appeared before them and there was a great brilliance, and the shepherds were very frightened.

And the angel said: "Do not be afraid. I bring you wonderful news. Today in David's city a Saviour has been born for you. He is Christ the Lord. You will find him wrapped up and lying in a manger."

At once there appeared with the angel a great throng of angels saying: "Glory to God in Heaven and on earth peace towards men who are good."

Then the angels left the shepherds, and the shepherds said to each other: "Let's hurry to Bethlehem and see this thing for ourselves."

THE SHEPHERDS' VISIT

ST. LUKE 2—1-20

And they travelled quickly and found Mary and Joseph and the baby lying in the manger. And having seen the baby they told everybody what had been told to them about the child, and then returned to their work marvelling at what had happened. And Mary cherished these memories in her heart.

SIMEON'S PROPHECY

ST. LUKE 2—21-35

When he was eight days old the baby was circumcised and named Jesus as the angel had instructed before his birth. And on his fortieth day he was taken to the Temple in Jerusalem in accordance with the custom of that time so that his parents could offer a sacrifice of two young pigeons or a pair of turtle doves.

There was in Jerusalem at that time a man called Simeon who was very devout. He was old, and he had been given a sign that he should not die before he had seen the Lord's Christ.

He was in the Temple when Joseph and Mary arrived with the baby Jesus. And immediately he took the child in his arms and said: "Now I can die in peace, for with my own eyes I have seen the light which you have sent to show truth to the Gentiles and bring glory to the people of Israel."

Mary and Joseph were amazed at this. Then Simeon turned to Mary and told her: "This child will decide the fates of many in Israel. But for you . . . you will suffer much sorrow."

THE WISE MEN'S VISIT:
AND THE RAGE OF HEROD

ST. MATTHEW 2—1-23

A short while after Jesus's birth, a party of astrologers came from the east travelling towards Jerusalem and asking everyone they met: "Where is the child who is born to be King of the Jews? We saw his star in the east and are following it. We have come to pay our respects."

When King Herod heard about this he was very worried, and invited the professors to meet him in private to find out what they knew. And he told them: "Search for this child carefully, and when you have found him let me know, so that I too can visit him and worship him."

The wise men left the king and headed for Bethlehem, for the star was now immediately ahead of them and they followed it until it led them to the place where Jesus lay. And as soon as they saw Jesus with his mother Mary they went down on their knees to worship him, and then they gave him the gifts they had brought . . . gold, incense and myrrh.

When the time came for them to leave, they returned to their own country by a different route for they had been warned in a dream that they should not visit Herod again.

And when they had left, the angel of the Lord

appeared to Joseph in a dream and told him, "Get up, and take Jesus and Mary to Egypt, and stay there as long as I tell you to for Herod will try to kill Jesus."

Joseph got up straight away and in the middle of the night set off for Egypt with Mary and Jesus.

25

When Herod realised that the wise men had tricked him he was furious, and issued instructions for every boy child under the age of two in and around Bethlehem to be killed. And this was done.

Some time later Herod died and an angel again came to Joseph in a dream and told him that it was safe to return to Israel. Joseph did so, taking Mary and Jesus but learned that Herod's son Archelaus was now ruler of Judea, so he went instead to Nazareth in the district of Galilee.

Here the child grew up, strong, wise and good.

JESUS AND THE TEMPLE ELDERS

ST. LUKE 2—41-50

When Jesus was twelve years old, he went with his parents to Jerusalem for the annual Passover celebration. When it was over Joseph and Mary headed back for home with a large group of travellers and had journeyed for a whole day before they realised that Jesus wasn't with them. They looked for him amongst the company but found he wasn't there, so they turned back towards Jerusalem. On the third day they found him in the Temple surrounded by teachers, asking them questions and answering their questions. People watching were amazed at his cleverness, including Mary and Joseph who could hardly believe their eyes.

29

Mary, still upset by how worried she had been, said, "My son, why have you done this? We have been looking everywhere for you. Your father and I were desperately worried."

And Jesus replied, "Didn't you know that I have work to do for my Father?"

They didn't understand him at all but Mary remembered these sayings and often thought about them.

CHAPTER TWO

JOHN THE BAPTIST MEETS JESUS

ST. MATTHEW 3—1-17
ST. MARK 1—4-11
ST. LUKE 3—1-18, 21-22
ST. JOHN 1—19-34

Now many years later it so happened that John (son of Elisabeth and Zacharias) arrived preaching in the Judean desert. He wore rough clothes of camel hair with a simple leather thong tied around his waist, and lived on locusts and honey. People flocked to him from miles around, publicly confessed their sins and were baptised in the River Jordan at Bethany. They called him John the Baptist.

33

John would tell the people, "It is true that I baptise you with water but that alone is not enough. Make sure that *you* change your way of life and turn over a new leaf. The man who has two shirts must give one to the man who has nothing. The man who has food must share his with the man who is without food."

He warned the tax-collectors to take only the correct amount of taxes, and the soldiers to be honest and not bully people.

Some people talked about John and thought that he might be Christ. But he told them, "Another will come, who is stronger than I, in fact I am not good enough to untie his shoe laces."

Then Jesus came to be baptised by John.

"Surely it is I who should be baptised by you," said John. But Jesus insisted that John baptise him and this was done.

And as he came up out of the water the sky opened and the Spirit of God came down like a dove and settled upon him and a voice from heaven said, "This is my beloved son, in whom I am well pleased. Listen to what he has to say."

34

THE TEMPTATION IN THE DESERT

ST. MATTHEW 4—1-11
ST. MARK 1—12-13
ST. LUKE 4—1-13
ST. JOHN 1—32-34

Then the Spirit of God sent him out into the desert to be tempted by the Devil. He was alone, and ate nothing for forty days and forty nights.

Then the Devil came to him and said, "If you are the Son of God take these stones and turn them into bread."

Jesus refused.

Then the Devil took Jesus to Jerusalem and took him to the highest ledge of the Temple there and said, "If you are the Son of God throw yourself down from here and see if the angels save you."

Again Jesus refused.

Then the Devil took Jesus to the top of a very high mountain and pointed to all the kingdoms of the world and said, "See all this. I will give it all to you if you will worship me."

And Jesus replied, "We have been taught that we must only worship God."

   And the Devil went away, and the angels came to
Jesus and cared for him.

CHAPTER THREE

JOHN IMPRISONED

ST. LUKE 3—19-20

Round about this time Herod the Tetrarch (a descendant of King Herod) who had been criticised by John for many evil acts, retaliated by putting John in prison.

JESUS BEGINS HIS MINISTRY

ST. MATTHEW 4—12-17
ST. MARK 1—14-15
ST. LUKE 4—14-15

When Jesus heard the news of John's arrest he went to live in Capernaum, a town on the edge of a lake, and he began to preach. He was about thirty years old.

"Change your hearts," he told people. "For the kingdom of heaven has arrived."

Very quickly Jesus became famous throughout Syria for his teaching that the kingdom of God had arrived. He healed the sick, and people who were ill were brought to him. Wherever he went he was followed by huge crowds and everybody praised him.

46

JOHN'S QUESTION

ST. MATTHEW 11—2-6
ST. LUKE 7—18-23

Reports of what Jesus was doing reached the ears of John the Baptist in prison and he called two of his disciples and gave them a message to take to Jesus.

"Are you the one we have been waiting for, or are we to go on waiting for someone else?"

The disciples went to Jesus and put this question to him, and he replied, "Go back to John and tell him what you have seen and heard. That the blind are made to see, cripples walk, lepers are healed, the deaf are made to hear, and dead men are restored to life. The good news is being given to those who need it. And happy is the man who does not lose faith in me."

JESUS RECRUITS HIS DISCIPLES

ST. MATTHEW 4—18-22
ST. MARK 1—16-20
ST. LUKE 5—1-11

One day Jesus was walking by the lake of Galilee when he saw two fishermen, Simon Peter and Andrew who were brothers, casting their net into the water.

"Come with me," he said, "and I will show you how to catch men."

So they left their nets and went with him. A little further on he met two more men, James and John, who were also brothers, mending their nets on a fishing boat, with their father Zebedee. He called to them and they left their father and their boat and went with him.

JESUS CALLS NATHANAEL

Then Jesus met Philip and said, "Follow me." Philip who came from the same town as Simon Peter and Andrew, had a friend called Nathanael (sometimes called Bartholomew) and he told him, "We have found the one Moses and the prophets wrote about. He is Jesus, son of Joseph. He comes from Nazareth."

"Can anything special come from such an insignificant place as Nazareth?" asked Nathanael sceptically.

"Come and meet him for yourself," said Philip.

When Jesus saw them coming, he said, "Here is a true Israelite. An honest man."

"Do you know me then?" asked Nathanael.

"Before Philip came to call you," said Jesus. "I saw you under a fig tree."

Nathanael was astonished. "Teacher, you really are the Son of God, King of Israel," he said.

Jesus replied, "What, just because I said that I saw you under a fig tree? I assure you that's nothing to what you will see. I promise you, you will see heaven wide open and God's angels ascending and descending around the Son of Man."

JESUS CHANGES WATER INTO WINE

ST. JOHN 2—1-10

Jesus, his mother and his disciples were guests at a wedding at Cana in Galilee. During the festivities Jesus's mother turned to him and said, "They have run out of wine, it is all used up."

"Why tell me?" said Jesus. But nevertheless his mother turned to the servants and said "Do whatever he tells you."

Nearby were standing six stone jars used to hold water for the Jewish purification rites. They were large jars. Each could hold twenty or thirty gallons.

"Fill them with water," Jesus instructed and they were filled to the brim. "Now draw some out and take it to the wine steward." This they did; the steward tasted the water and it had changed into wine.

He, of course, had no idea where it had come from, but said to Jesus, "At most parties the host gives people the best wine first and saves the cheaper stuff until they've had plenty to drink. But you have kept the best wine until now."

Only the servants and the disciples knew what Jesus had done. The servants did not understand. The disciples knew, and believed in him.

54

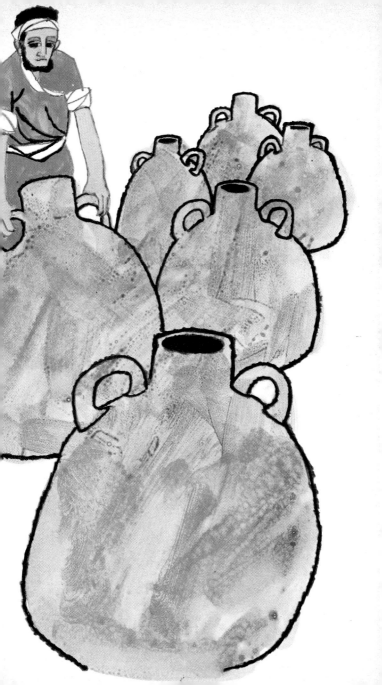

JESUS HEALS THE SICK

ST. MARK 1—21-28
ST. LUKE 4—31-37

They went to Capernaum. On the Sabbath Jesus entered the synagogue and started to teach. Everybody was astonished by the knowledgeable way he spoke.

A mad man came near to Jesus, shouting at him. Jesus spoke sharply to the evil spirit inside the man. "Get out of him."

The evil spirit gave a loud scream and left the man, and the man was calm and no longer mad.

Of course this astonished the people who were watching even further.

57

Jesus left the synagogue and went to Simon Peter
and Andrew's house, with James and John. When he
arrived there he learned that Simon Peter's mother-in-
law was ill in bed. He went to her, and taking her hand
helped her to her feet. Immediately the fever left her.

Throughout the evening the people of the town were
gathering at the door of the house, bringing to him all
their sick friends and relatives, and he healed many.

58

Early in the morning, before it was light, Jesus left the house and went to a deserted place and prayed. Simon Peter and the others looked for him, and when they found him they told him that everybody was looking for him.

"Then we shall go to other towns, so that I can give my message to other people," said Jesus. "That is what I am here for."

59

JESUS AND THE LEPER

ST. MATTHEW 8—1-4
ST. MARK 1—40-45
ST. LUKE 5—12-16

One day a man came to him who was covered with the sores of leprosy. He knelt before Jesus, imploring, "Please cure me."

And Jesus was filled with pity for the man, and touched him, saying, "Be clean."

At once the man's leprosy vanished, and Jesus told him to go straight away and show himself to the priest at the Temple, but to tell nobody else about it.

But the man went away and talked to a great many people about what had happened to him and consequently Jesus became so famous that he had to stay outside the towns, but still the people managed to find him.

THE SOLDIER'S SERVANT

ST. MATTHEW 8—5-13
ST. LUKE 7—1-30

One day a Roman soldier approached him. "Sir, my servant is paralysed and in terrible pain," he said.

"I will come and heal him," replied Jesus.

But the soldier said, "Just give the order, and my servant will recover. It is not important enough for you to travel to my house. Your order will cure him."

Jesus was astonished at the man's great faith, and he said to the Roman soldier, "Go home and everything will be as you believe."

And the servant was healed immediately.

61

THE PARALYSED MAN

ST. MATTHEW 9—1-8
ST. MARK 2—1-12
ST. LUKE 5—17-26

One day when he was at Capernaum a rumour spread that he was in a certain house. Such a huge crowd collected that it was impossible to reach the doorway. A group of four arrived, carrying between them a paralysed man. They realised that they could not get to Jesus through the vast crowd, so they climbed onto the roof, removed some tiles and let down the paralytic on his bed through the hole in the roof.

Jesus, seeing their faith, said to the man on the bed, "My son, your sins are forgiven."

Some scribes, overhearing this were offended and thought, "This is blasphemy. Only God can forgive sins."

Jesus knew what they were thinking and said to them, "What do you think means more to a paralysed man? To say 'your sins are forgiven' or to say 'pick up your bed and walk'? But to prove that I have authority to forgive sins on earth, I say (and he turned to the paralysed man) 'Stand up, pick up your bed and walk home.'"

Then the man sprang to his feet, took up his bed and walked away, watched by everyone.

JESUS TELLS: WHY I AM HERE

ST. MATTHEW 9—9-13
ST. MARK 2—13-17
ST. LUKE 5—27-32

In the course of his day-to-day life, Jesus met Matthew who was a tax-collector. "Follow me," said Jesus, and Matthew left his desk and followed him. Later they were having dinner at Matthew's house with Jesus's disciples and many other tax-collectors and disreputable characters were there. The scribes and Pharisees saw what was happening and they asked the disciples, "Why does he eat and drink with these awful people?"

But Jesus overheard and he said: "The healthy don't need a doctor, but the sick do. I didn't come to guide the people who are good already, I came to guide the sinners."

64

THE TWELVE ARE CHOSEN

ST. MATTHEW 10—1- 4
ST. MARK 3—13-19
ST. LUKE 6—12-16

Jesus went up the hill and found a flat place and spent the night praying. When it was morning, he called his closest followers and chose from amongst them twelve men whom he could send out to preach and who would have the power to drive out evil spirits. The men were Simon Peter, James and John, Andrew, Philip, Bartholomew, Matthew, Thomas, James (son of Alphaeus), Thaddaeus, Simon and Judas Iscariot who became a traitor.

CHAPTER FOUR

THE SERMON ON THE MOUNT

ST. MATTHEW 5, 6 and 7

They sat down together, and Jesus spoke to them. "Those who are humble shall be given heaven.

Those who are sad shall be given courage and comfort.

Those who are patient shall be given the earth.

Those who look for goodness will be given it.

Those who show mercy to others will receive mercy.

Those who are honest in their hearts will see God.

Those who make peace shall be known as the sons of God. And those who have been persecuted for their goodness shall be given heaven.

If you are wronged by others because you support me, be glad, for your reward in heaven will be truly wonderful.

Men do not light a lamp then hide it under a bucket. They put the lamp where everyone can see it, and where it can give light for others to see by. Let your light shine like that. Let men see the good things you do and praise your Father in heaven.

You have heard the saying 'An eye for an eye, a tooth for a tooth.' Well I say if a man hits your right cheek, turn your left cheek as well. You have heard it said 'Love your neighbour and hate your enemy.' Well I say love your enemies as well, for God makes the sun rise for evil men as well as good, and sends his rain upon honest men as well as dishonest.

Do not show off when you are doing a good deed. If you give money to charity do so in secret. Your Father knows all secrets and will reward you.

When you pray do so in the privacy of your own room, with the door closed. And pray like this:

'Our Father who art in heaven, we must honour your name. May your kingdom come, and your wishes be carried out on earth as they are in heaven.

Give us each day enough food.

And forgive us when we do something wrong towards you, as we forgive those who wrong us.

Protect us from temptation, and save us from evil.'

Don't hoard treasures on earth where they can go rusty and moth-eaten. Keep your treasure safe in heaven. Don't worry about living, what you are going to eat or drink or wear. Your heavenly Father knows that you need food and drink and clothes and he will provide them. The one who asks will always have it given to him, in the same way as the one who is looking will always find what he is looking for.

Behave towards others as you would like them to behave towards yourself.

Be on your guard against dishonest teachers who come dressed as sheep but are really wolves in disguise.

And having heard my words, pay attention to them. For to ignore them would be like the man who built his house on sand, and when the rain, floods and wind came the house was battered down because its foundations were inadequate.''

CHAPTER FIVE

JESUS EXPLAINS

ST. MATTHEW 9—14-17
ST. MARK 2—18-22
ST. LUKE 5—33-39

One day John's disciples asked Jesus, "We and the Pharisees fast, but your disciples do nothing of the sort. Why should this be?"

And Jesus replied, "Would guests at a wedding fast whilst the bridegroom was there? The day will come when the bridegroom is taken away from them and they will fast then."

73

JESUS CALMS THE STORM

ST. MATTHEW 8—23-27
ST. MARK 4—35-41
ST. LUKE 8—22-25

Jesus and his disciples were aboard a boat crossing the lake, when a fierce storm blew up, rocking the boat and sending the waves pounding over its decks. Jesus was asleep, and his disciples woke him crying "Lord, save us, for we are drowning."

Jesus stood up. "Be quiet," he said to the wind and the waves, and the wind dropped and the water was calm.

Then he turned to his disciples, "What has happened to your faith," he said. "Why are you so frightened?"

And they were astonished and asked themselves "What kind of a man is this who can tell the wind and the waves what to do and they obey him?"

THE GERASENE MANIAC

ST. MATTHEW 8—28-34
ST. MARK 5—1-20
ST. LUKE 8—26-39

When they arrived at the far side of the Lake at Gerasene a mad man appeared from among the tombs. He was an outcast, who screamed day and night and stuck jagged stones into himself. As soon as he saw Jesus he ran to him and knelt, shouting, "What have you got to do with me Jesus, son of the most High God. For God's sake, don't torture me."

"What is your name?" asked Jesus.

"Legion," the mad man replied, "meaning there are many inside me."

Nearby a herd of pigs was grazing on the hillside, and Jesus instructed the evil spirits to leave the man and go into the pigs. And immediately the herd of pigs went mad and stampeded over the cliff top into the water below and were drowned.

And the man who had been mad was now sane and calm.

And when the people in the town saw what had happened they were afraid and begged Jesus to go away.

THE DEATH OF JOHN THE BAPTIST

ST. MATTHEW 14—3-13
ST. MARK 6—17-29

John the Baptist was still chained in prison for having dared to criticise Herod, in particular he had publicly condemned Herod for marrying his own brother's wife, Herodias. Herodias wanted John the Baptist killed for this, but Herod was afraid to go too far, knowing that John was a good and holy man.

Then it was Herod's birthday and he gave a great party for all the important people in his court, and the officers in his army, and the most influential people in Galilee. During the celebrations the daughter of Herodias came into the banquet room and danced for the guests, who were so delighted with her performance that Herod promised her: "Ask for whatever you like and I shall give it to you . . . half my kingdom if you want it."

Well the girl went outside and asked her mother what should she say. And her mother replied, "Ask for the head of John the Baptist."

So the girl went back into the banquet room and said to Herod, "I want you to give me John the Baptist's head at once, on a dish."

The king was very upset by the turn of events, but having made such a sweeping promise so publicly he felt he could not break his word. Turning to one of his bodyguards he instructed him to bring John's head. The soldier went straight away to the prison, beheaded the prisoner John and returned with his head on a dish which he gave to the girl. And she gave it to her mother.

Later John's disciples heard about this and took his body and laid it in a tomb. Then they went to Jesus to tell him what had happened, and when he had listened to their news he went away by boat to a quiet place where he was alone.

JESUS INSTRUCTS THE TWELVE

ST. MATTHEW 10
ST. MARK 6—7-13
ST. LUKE 9—1-6

Then Jesus called the twelve disciples together and sent them off in pairs with these instructions: "Concentrate on the lost sheep of the house of Israel. Tell them that the kingdom of heaven has arrived. Heal the sick, restore the dead to life. Take no money with you, carry no food for the journey, nor even a change of clothes.

"When you enter a house, give it your blessing. But if people will not welcome you, nor even listen to you, then don't waste your time on them."

So they went on their way, preaching and healing.

HEROD'S FEARS

ST. MATTHEW 14—1-2
ST. MARK 6—14-16
ST. LUKE 9—7-9

Some people believed that Jesus was Elijah, and others believed that Jesus was one of the old prophets restored to life again. News of what Jesus was doing reached the ears of Herod who found the stories alarming. "It must be John, risen from the dead," he thought. And he was anxious to see Jesus for himself.

81

THE FEEDING OF THE FIVE THOUSAND

ST. MATTHEW 14—13-33
ST. MARK 6—30-52
ST. LUKE 9—10-17
ST. JOHN 6—1-21

When the disciples returned from their travels they wanted to tell Jesus of their experiences so they all went with him to a town called Bethsaida, to talk privately. But the people from the neighbouring towns and villages found out where he was and clamoured to follow him.

Jesus took pity on them because he thought they were like sheep without a shepherd, so throughout the day he talked to them and healed them until it was quite late. Then his disciples said, "You must be very tired, you have not eaten. Send the people away, they can buy food from the farms."

Jesus replied, "There's no need for that. You feed them."

The disciples were dismayed for there were five thousand people in the crowd. "How are we to do that?" they asked Jesus.

"Go and see how much food you have," said Jesus, and they did, and they told him that they had found a boy who had five loaves of bread and two fishes.

Then Jesus told them to make all the people sit down, in groups, and when this had been done, he took the five loaves and the two fishes, raised his eyes to heaven and blessed the food. Then he broke the bread, and the fishes and handed the pieces to the disciples to share among the people.

Everyone ate as much as he or she wanted and when they had all finished the disciples collected the leftover scraps and filled twelve baskets full.

JESUS WALKS ON THE WATER

ST. MATTHEW 14—13-33
ST. MARK 6—30-52
ST. LUKE 9—10-17
ST. JOHN 6—1-21

While Jesus was sending the crowds home, he told the disciples to go on ahead to the other side of the lake. When he was ready to join them he could see that they were exhausted with rowing against the wind, and he went out to join them, walking on the water. When they saw this ghostly figure walking on the lake they were terrified, but he told them "Don't be afraid, it is I, Jesus."

"Lord, if it is really you, make me come to you on the water too," said Simon Peter.

"Come on then," Jesus replied. And Simon Peter stepped down from the boat and started to walk towards Jesus but when he realised what he was doing and saw the fierce waves he lost his nerve and began to sink, crying for help and saying "Lord, save me."

And Jesus stretched out his hand and saved him. "Why did you panic," he asked. "What happened to your faith?"

They both climbed into the boat then the wind dropped and the disciples knelt before Jesus and said, "You are indeed the Son of God."

84

THE MAN WITH THE WITHERED HAND: AND THE PLOT TO DESTROY JESUS

ST. MATTHEW 12—9-14
ST. MARK 3—1-6
ST. LUKE 6—6-11

Jesus went into the synagogue one Sabbath day to teach, and there was a man there with a withered hand. The scribes and the Pharisees were watching Jesus to see if he would break their Sabbath laws by curing the man. They were hoping for some evidence to use against him in this respect. But Jesus knew exactly what was going on in their minds and he called the man to stand up and walk into the middle of the synagogue. Then he pointed to the man and he said to the scribes and Pharisees, "Is it against the law on the Sabbath day to do good, or bad? To save life or to kill?" Nobody answered him, and he said "If you had a sheep which fell into a ditch on the Sabbath day, surely you would pull it out. Isn't a man's life more valuable than a sheep's?"

Obstinately they did not answer and Jesus looked angrily at them all. Then he said to the man "Stretch out your hand."

The man put out his withered hand, and it was healed.

Then the Pharisees left the synagogue and at once teamed up with Herod's supporters to plot a way of destroying Jesus.

THE CURE OF THE DEAF MUTE

ST. MARK 7—31-37

One day Jesus was preaching to a crowd when some people pushed a way through bringing a man who was deaf and dumb, asking Jesus to heal the man. He took the man away from the crowd to where it was quiet, put his fingers into the man's ears, and touched the man's tongue with spittle. Then, looking up to heaven he said, "Be opened."

And at once the man's ears were "opened" and he could hear, and at the same time he could speak. Jesus told the crowd not to discuss what had happened, but they were so full of admiration and wonder that they went away and told everybody.

THE BLIND MAN OF BETHSAIDA

ST. MARK 8—22-26

Arriving at the town of Bethsaida, Jesus was met by some people who had with them a blind man whom they begged him to heal. Jesus took the blind man by the hand and led him away from the houses. Then he put spittle on the blind man's eyes and, touching him, asked "Can you see anything?"

The man replied "I can see people who look like trees, walking about." Then Jesus laid his hands on the man's eyes a second time, whereupon the man could see everything clearly and distinctly, and he was cured.

87

JAIRUS'S DAUGHTER:
AND THE WOMAN IN THE CROWD

ST. MATTHEW 9—18-26
ST. MARK 5—21-43
ST. LUKE 8—40-56

Jesus was preaching beside the lake, surrounded by many people, when a man called Jairus, an official at the synagogue, pushed his way through to Jesus and fell on his knees imploring "My little girl is desperately ill. Please come at once."

Jesus proceeded to follow Jairus to the house where the child lay, but the crowd was thick and he had to battle his way through. Among the people who had come to see him that day was a woman who had suffered from a bleeding disease for twelve years. She had suffered all sorts of painful treatments, and had spent all her money on doctors' bills, and was getting steadily worse. She had heard about Jesus and had come to see him and now she squeezed her way through the crowd and stretched out her hand for she felt that if she could only touch some part of him she would get well.

And as her fingers touched his cloak, the bleeding inside her ceased, and she knew that she was cured. But Jesus stopped.

"Who touched me?" he asked.

His disciples said, "People are touching you all the time . . . look at the crowd pushing."

But Jesus said "Somebody touched me, I felt power going from me." And as he continued to look around the woman came forward, frightened and trembling, and she fell at his feet and told him the truth.

And Jesus told her, "My daughter, your faith has cured you."

Whilst he was still talking to her, some people arrived from Jairus's house to say that Jairus's daughter had died.

"It's too late to do anything to help her," they said. "Don't waste Jesus's time."

But Jesus overheard this and he said to Jairus, "Have faith," then hurried to the house where there was a great deal of weeping and wailing going on.

"Be quiet and go outside," he told them. "The child is not dead, she is asleep." Some of the onlookers laughed scornfully at this, but nevertheless they went outside and Jesus allowed only the parents of the child, and Simon Peter, James and James' brother John to remain.

Then he went to the bed where the child lay, and taking her hand he said, "Little girl, do as I say, and get up."

And she got up at once and began to walk about. Her parents were amazed and overjoyed, and Jesus told them to give her something to eat.

THE WIDOW OF NAIN

ST. LUKE 7—11-17

Jesus went to a town called Nain, accompanied by his disciples and followed by a great crowd of people. And as he approached the town gates he passed a funeral procession, and the dead man was the only son of a widow who was deeply distressed. Jesus felt sorry for her.

"Don't cry," he said. Then he went to the stand on which the corpse was being carried. The bearers stood still, and Jesus said, "Young man I tell you to get up."

And the dead man sat up and started talking and Jesus had given the widow back her son.

The people were overawed and praised God. "He has sent a great leader to us," they said and as the stories about Jesus were told throughout the land, many people had the same opinion.

THE BENT WOMAN

ST. LUKE 13—10-17

One Sabbath day when he was teaching in a synagogue, he saw a woman who was bent double and couldn't stand upright. She had suffered this deformity for eighteen years. Jesus called her to him and said, "Woman, you are cured." He put his hands on her, and she at once stood up straight, and praised God.

But the synagogue official who had seen what happened was indignant and spoke to all the people saying, "God gave us six days for work. If you want to be healed come on one of those work days and not on the Sabbath."

Then Jesus answered him. "Hypocrites," he said. "Is there one person here who does not untie his ox on the Sabbath so that the animal can drink water. And this woman has been tied for eighteen years, isn't it right to untie her bonds on the Sabbath?"

His enemies found all this very confusing and embarrassing, but the people were overjoyed at the marvellous things he did.

THE EPILEPTIC

ST. MATTHEW 17—14-20
ST. MARK 9—14-29
ST. LUKE 9—37-43

One day when Jesus's disciples were preaching to the crowd, Jesus approached and saw that an argument was going on. As soon as they saw him, the people surged towards him.

"Why are you arguing?" he asked.

A man from the crowd answered, "Master I have an only son. There is an evil spirit inside him, it has made him dumb and sometimes it makes him fall to the ground, foam at the mouth and grind his teeth. His body goes rigid. I brought him here, and asked your disciples to cast out the evil spirit but they cannot."

"You faithless lot," said Jesus. "How much longer must I put up with you?"

They brought the boy forward and as soon as he stood before Jesus he fell to the ground, writhing, foaming at the mouth.

"How long has he had this condition?" Jesus asked the father, who replied "Since childhood. Sometimes the evil spirit has thrown the boy into fire or water in an effort to destroy him. Please take pity on us and help."

"Everything is possible if you have faith," said Jesus.

"I do have faith," cried the father of the boy.

Then Jesus rebuked the spirit. "Deaf and dumb spirit," he commanded, "come out at once and never enter this boy again."

At once the boy went into convulsions, shouting, then fell to the ground and lay so corpselike that some people thought he was dead. Jesus took him by the hand, helped him to his feet and he was cured.

The disciples, when they were alone with him, asked Jesus, "Why couldn't we cure the boy?"

And he answered, "Because you don't have enough faith. I tell you that if your faith was the size of a mustard seed you could say to a mountain 'Move from here to there' and it would move. With faith nothing would be impossible for you.

ST. LUKE 17—5-6

Were your faith the size of a mustard seed you could say to this mulberry tree 'Be uprooted and planted in the sea' and it would obey you."

THE TEN LEPERS

ST. LUKE 17—11-19

One day as Jesus was approaching a village he heard voices calling him and saw, standing a distance away, ten lepers.

"Jesus, Master take pity on us," they shouted.

Jesus replied, "Go and show yourselves to the priest," and as they turned away to do as he had told them, their sores disappeared and they were cured.

One of them, a Samaritan, realising that he was well, turned back and threw himself at the feet of Jesus and thanked him.

"Where are the others?" said Jesus. "Weren't all ten of you cured? Where are the other nine? It seems that the only one who has bothered to thank God is this foreigner."

Then he told the man, "Go on your way . . . your faith has saved you."

95

THE BLIND BEGGAR

ST. JOHN 9—1-34

One day Jesus saw a blind beggar, the man had been born blind and many people said that his blindness was God's way of punishing the parents' sins. But Jesus said, "His parents did not sin, this man's blindness is an opportunity for God's work to be displayed."

And with these words he spat on the ground, mixed some spittle and earth into a paste and put this on the blind man's eyes. Then he told him to go and wash in a nearby pool. The blind man did so and immediately could see.

Then neighbours who had known him said, "Surely this isn't the same man who used to sit and beg?" Some said it was the same man, others said it was a man who looked like him.

But the man, hearing the speculations, said, "I am that man."

So they asked him, "Then how is it you are no longer blind?" And he told them what Jesus had done.

So they took the man to the Pharisees, and he repeated his story about Jesus. The Pharisees were divided amongst themselves. Those who knew that Jesus had cured the man on the Sabbath were very angry. Others refused to believe that the man had ever been blind in the first place so they sent for his parents to check his story.

His parents were afraid of the synagogue leaders who had already threatened to expel anybody who said that Jesus was Christ. So when the Pharisees asked them how the blindness was cured they replied, "This is our son. He was born blind. Now he can see. As to how he was cured, you'd better ask him. He's old enough to speak for himself."

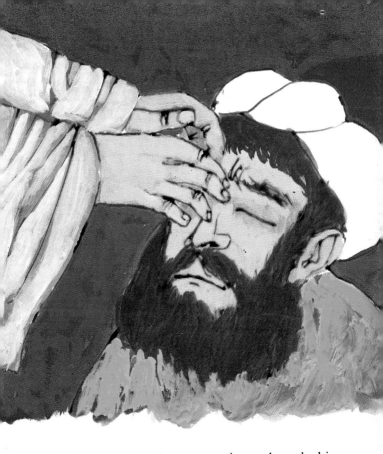

So they sent for the man again, and made him repeat his story, going over all the details. And they said to him, "We know that God spoke to Moses, but as for this man Jesus, we don't know where he comes from."

And the man replied, "You astonish me. Since the beginning of the world it has been unheard of for a blind man to see. If this man Jesus is not from God, how could he do this?"

At this the Pharisees were furious and drove the man away.

MIRACLE AT BETHZATHA:
AND THE ANGER OF THE JEWS

ST. JOHN 5—1-18

In Jerusalem there was a sheep pool surrounded by five arches and the place was called Bethzatha. Under these arches there were always a great many sick people, blind, lame, paralysed, waiting for the water to move for there was a tradition that from time to time an angel would come down and move the waters of the pool, and that the first person to enter the waters after they had been disturbed in this manner would be cured.

Jesus was visiting Jerusalem for one of the religious festivals, and noticed a man lying at Bethzatha, and the man had been waiting there for thirty-eight years.

Knowing this, Jesus asked him, "Do you want to get well again?"

"Sir," said the sick man, "I have nobody to lift me into the pool when the water is stirred up. By the time I get to the pool somebody else has already managed to get into the water before me."

"Get up," said Jesus. "Pick up your sleeping mat, and walk." At once the man recovered, picked up his sleeping mat and walked away.

It was the Sabbath day, and certain Jews said to the man, "You know you shouldn't be carrying your sleeping mat on the Sabbath."

"The man who cured me told me to carry it," he replied.

"Who is the man who told you this?" they asked, but he had no idea who it was for Jesus had slipped away into the dense crowd the moment the man was well.

But later that day Jesus met him again, in the Temple. "Now that you are a fit man," he said, "be careful not to sin again for something worse might happen to you."

Then the man went to the Jews who had questioned him and told them that the one who had cured him was Jesus.

The Jews were opposed to Jesus because he did these things on the Sabbath. Jesus's reply to this attitude was to say, "My Father goes on working, and so do I."

And this made the Jews even more determined to kill him because not only did he break their Sabbath laws but he referred to God as his own Father and so put himself on equal terms with God.

CHAPTER SIX

JESUS TEACHES

ST. MATTHEW 13—1-9
ST. MARK 4—1-9
ST. LUKE 8—4-8

Often when Jesus taught the people, he told them "parables" or picture stories to help them understand his preachings.

A large crowd gathered around Jesus, so large in fact that he climbed into a boat in order to be able to speak to them all, and they sat or stood on the beach listening to him.

THE PARABLE OF THE SEEDS

ST. MATTHEW 13—1-9
ST. MARK 4—1-9
ST. LUKE 8—4-8

"Imagine," said Jesus, "a farmer going out to sow some seeds. As he worked some seeds fell on the edge of the path where they were quickly eaten up by the birds. Some seeds fell on the stones and rocks where there was a little soil. They sprang up but as soon as the sun shone they withered and, having weak roots, died. Others fell among thorns and weeds and were choked. Others fell on rich soil and these grew strong and healthy and produced a rich crop."

THE PARABLE OF THE SEEDS
EXPLAINED

ST. MATTHEW 13—18-23
ST. MARK 4—13-20
ST. LUKE 8—11-15

Then he explained the meaning of this story to his disciples. For the seed, he said, was the word of God. Those on the edge of the path are people who hear the word but before it takes root in their heart the Devil comes and carries it off. The man who hears it on the rocky ground is the one who welcomes it, but his enthusiasm doesn't last and the first time he is put to the test the word withers and dies because it has no roots in him. The one who receives it in the thorns and weeds, is the one who hears the word but is more concerned with the material things of life, and the word is choked by the lure of riches. And the one who receives the word in rich soil is the one who hears and truly understands and shares his harvest with others.

THE GOOD SAMARITAN

ST. LUKE 10—25-37

On one occasion when Jesus was preaching to a large crowd, a young lawyer who thought he could trick Jesus, stood up and asked "What must I do to be sure of eternal life?"

"What does the Law tell you, and what have you learned from your reading?" asked Jesus.

The young man replied, "It is written that I must love God with all my heart, with all my soul and with all my strength. And I must love my neighbour as much as I love myself."

"That's right," said Jesus. "Well if you follow those rules, you can be sure of eternal life."

But the man pressed the point further. "Who is my neighbour?" he asked.

Then Jesus told him a story.

A man was travelling from Jerusalem to Jericho, along a lonely road, when he was attacked by a gang of robbers who beat him almost to death and escaped with all his money.

A priest happened to be travelling along the same road, and when he saw the man's beaten body lying by the roadside, he crossed to the other side of the road and passed by without stopping. Some time afterwards one of the Temple assistants also came along the road, and seeing the injured man he too crossed over and passed on the other side.

Then a third man came along, a Samaritan. When he saw the man lying there, he felt very sorry for him. Kneeling down he washed his wounds with the oil and wine which he was carrying and bandaged them. Then he lifted the man onto his own horse and took him to the nearest inn. He gave the innkeeper some money and instructed him, "Look after this man. On my return journey I will call in and if you have had any additional expense I will make it good."

Then Jesus turned to the young lawyer and said, "Which of the three men proved to be a neighbour to the man who had been attacked?"

"Why, the one who took pity on him," said the lawyer.

"Then go and do the same," replied Jesus.

107

JESUS SAYS : DON'T BE AFRAID TO ASK

ST. LUKE 11—5-13

Another time Jesus said, "Imagine a man goes to his friend in the middle of the night, knocking at the door and asking 'A guest has just arrived at my house and I have no food for him. Please lend me some bread.' And the man inside replies, 'Go away, we're all in bed and the door is bolted.'

"Well if that man who wants to borrow some bread persists, knocking at the door and refusing to go away without it, his friend will eventually have to give in, not out of friendship but simply to get rid of the man outside. And he will get up and give the man what he wants.

And this is what you should do. You should ask, and it will be given to you. Knock and the door will be opened. The one who searches always finds. No father would give his child a stone when it asks for bread, or hand him a snake when he asks for fish. So if earthly fathers have that much feeling for their children, imagine how much more benevolent God is, and how eager to give the Holy Spirit to those who ask for it."

PICTURES OF HEAVEN

ST. MATTHEW 13—31-32
ST. MARK 4—30-32
ST. LUKE 13—18-19

Jesus was describing to the crowd what was meant by the kingdom of heaven.

"It is like a mustard seed," he said, "which a man took and planted in a field. The mustard seed is the smallest of all seeds, but when it grows it is the biggest of all the shrubs and sends out strong branches and the birds come and make their nests in it."

ST. MATTHEW 13—44-46

Then he said, "The kingdom of heaven is like treasure hidden in a field. A man discovers the buried treasure, hides it again then goes away and sells everything he owns so that he can buy the field.

"Again, the kingdom of heaven is like the merchant who is looking for fine pearls. When he finds what he is looking for, a pearl of great value, he sells everything he owns in order to buy it."

PARABLE OF THE WEEDS

"You could say that the kingdom of heaven is like the man who sowed good seed in his field. Then when everybody was asleep his enemy crept into the field and sowed weeds among the wheat, then went away.

"The new wheat sprouted but so did the weeds and the man's servants said, "That must have been poor quality seed.' But the man guessed what had happened. 'Some enemy has done this' he told them.

'Shall we go and weed it out?' said the servants. But that wasn't a practical idea. 'You might pull up the wheat with the weeds,' said the man.

'No, let them both grow until it is time for the harvest. Then the reapers can collect the weeds, tie them in bundles and burn them. And the wheat will be gathered and stored in my barn.' "

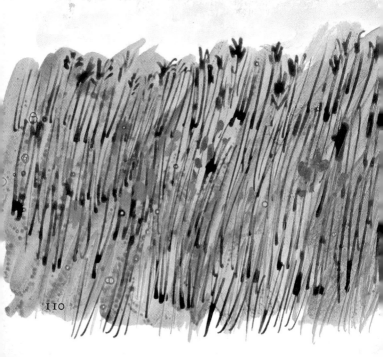

PARABLE OF THE WEEDS EXPLAINED

ST. MATTHEW 13—36-43

Turning to his disciples Jesus explained, "The man who sowed the good seeds is the Son of Man, the field is the world and the good seed is all the subjects of his kingdom. The man who crept into the field is the Devil and the weeds he sowed are the evil people. The harvest is the end of the world, and the reapers are the angels.

"Just as weeds are gathered up and burned, so those who defy God will be destroyed in a blazing fire. It will be too late for tears of regret.

"And the good will remain to shine out like the sun."

HEAVEN—AND A FISHING NET

ST. MATTHEW 13—47-50

"Similarly the kingdom of heaven is like a net thrown into the sea. When it is full the fishermen pull it in and once it is ashore they proceed to sort out their catch. They put the good fish into a basket and throw away those which aren't any good.

"And this is how it will be at the end of time, when the angels will separate the good from the bad, and throw the bad into the fire."

THE RICH MAN AND THE KINGDOM OF HEAVEN

ST. MATTHEW 19—16-26
ST. MARK 10—17-27
ST. LUKE 18—18-27

A rich young man came to Jesus and asked him, "What good deed must I do to inherit eternal life?"

Jesus replied, "You must not kill, you must not commit adultery, you must not steal, you must not lie, you must obey your mother and father and you must love your neighbour as much as you love yourself."

The young man said, "I have followed all these rules all my life. What else is there?"

And Jesus said, "If you want to be perfect, go and sell all your possessions and give the money to the poor, then you will have treasure in heaven. Come, follow me."

But the young man's face showed how disappointed he was to hear these words, and he went away.

And Jesus told his disciples, "It will be very hard for a rich man to enter the kingdom of heaven. In fact it would be easier for a camel to pass through the eye of a needle than for a rich man to enter the kingdom of heaven."

JESUS AND THE WOMAN'S TEARS

ST. LUKE 7—36-50

Jesus accepted an invitation to eat at the house of Simon the Pharisee. After he had taken his place at the table a woman came in, who had a bad reputation in the town. She had heard that Jesus would be spending the evening there, and brought with her an alabaster jar of ointment, then she knelt at his feet. As she waited she wept, and her tears fell onto Jesus's feet. And she wiped them away with her hair. And when she had dried his feet she gently rubbed the costly ointment onto them.

His host, Simon, seeing this, thought, "If this man had divine powers he would know that this is a bad woman whom he allows to touch him."

Jesus who knew Simon's thoughts, said, "Simon, I've something to say to you."

"Tell me, Master," said Simon.

And Jesus said, "There was a man who was owed money by two others. One of them owed him five hundred pieces of silver and the other owed him fifty pieces of silver. Both were unable to pay him the money they owed him, so he excused them both. Which one do you suppose loved him most for this kindness?"

"Why the one who had owed him the greater amount of money, I suppose," said Simon.

"You are right," said Jesus. He turned to the woman. "Simon," he said, "you see this woman don't you? I came into your house and you did not offer to wash my feet, but she has washed my feet with her tears and dried them with her hair. You did not kiss me, but she has been showering my feet with kisses ever since I arrived. You didn't give me oil for my head, but she put ointment on my feet.

"And that is how I know that her sins have been forgiven for that is why she has such love and gratitude to offer."

Then he said to the woman, "Your sins have been forgiven."

Then the guests at the table said to each other, "Who is he to forgive sins?"

But Jesus said to the woman, "It is your faith that has saved you. Go in peace."

JESUS JOURNEYS

ST. LUKE 8—1-3

Jesus visited every town and village preaching and telling people the good news about God's kingdom. He travelled with his twelve· disciples, and certain women whom he had healed, such as Mary Magdalene, Joanna (the wife of Herod's agent, Chuza), Susanna and several others who had money to help support him.

PARABLE OF THE LOST SHEEP

ST. MATTHEW 18—12-14
ST. LUKE 15—1-7

Jesus knew that the scribes and Pharisees complained that he spoke to tax-collectors and sinners, so to explain why he did this he told them the following parables.

"What man with a hundred sheep, having lost one of them would not leave the other ninety-nine and go searching for the missing one. And having found it put it joyfully on his shoulders and carry it home and call all his friends and neighbours for a celebration and say 'Isn't it marvellous, I've found my sheep that was lost.' In the same way there is more rejoicing in heaven over one sinner who repents than over ninety-nine good men who have no need of repentance."

PARABLE OF THE LOST COIN

ST. LUKE 15—8-10

"Take another example . . . what woman, with ten coins would not, if she lost one of them, light a lamp and sweep the house right through, and search thoroughly until she had found it. Then call her friends and neighbours and say 'Celebrate with me, I've found the money I lost.' In the same way there is rejoicing among God's angels over one repentant sinner."

PARABLE OF THE TWO SONS

ST. LUKE 15—11-32

Jesus also told the story of the two sons, one a spendthrift, the other dutiful. The younger son, who was the extravagant one, said to his father, "Father, let me have my share of the money which would eventually be left to me." So the father divided his property between the two sons and the younger one took his share and left for a foreign country where he promptly squandered it all on his own pleasures.

When it was all used up he was forced to look for work and got a job feeding pigs. He was so hungry he would willingly have eaten the pig's food, except that he wasn't allowed to. He was on the point of starvation and nobody would lift a finger to help him.

He remembered what it was like at his father's farm.

"My father's servants are better off than I am," he thought.

"They have more food than they can possibly eat. I will leave this place, and go home, and say to my father, 'Father, I don't deserve to be called your son, but may I stay with you as one of your paid servants?'"

So he went back to his father. When he was still some distance away his father saw him and was filled with pity. He ran to him, put his arms around him and kissed him.

"Father, I have sinned against heaven and against you," said the son. "I no longer deserve to be called your son."

But the father called to his servants, "Hurry, fetch the best clothes and put them on him. Put a ring on his finger and shoes on his feet. And get that calf we've been fattening up, and kill it and we'll have a feast and celebrate. For this is my son. I thought he was dead, but he's alive. He was lost, but I have found him."

Soon the party was in full swing and the elder son, on his way back from working in the fields, heard all the singing and dancing and seeing one of the servants asked him what was going on.

"Your brother has returned," said the servant. "And your father has killed the calf we'd fattened, because his son is home safe and sound."

The elder brother was very angry when he heard this and hung about outside the house refusing to go in. When his father came outside to persuade him in the elder son burst out angrily "All these years I've worked hard for you and never once disobeyed your orders, and all that time you never offered as much as a kid for me to celebrate with my friends. Yet your other son squanders your money on himself and his women and then comes back and you kill a calf for him."

The father replied, "My son, you have been with me always, and everything I have is yours. But how can we not show our joy now that your brother has returned? I thought he was dead, but here he is, alive. He was lost, and I have found him again."

THE RICH MAN AND THE PAUPER

ST. LUKE 16—19-31

Jesus told another parable. "There was a rich man who dressed in purple and fine linen and lived a life of luxury, feasting magnificently every day. And there was a poor dying man called Lazarus who was put down at the rich man's gate, incapable of moving any further even when the dogs came and licked his sores. He longed to be allowed to eat the scraps that fell from the rich man's table.

Then both men died. The poor man was carried away by angels to the protection of Abraham. The rich man was buried, and his spirit in the lower world looked up and saw Abraham a long way away, with Lazarus beside him. He cried out 'Abraham, pity me. Send Lazarus to dip his finger in cold water and put it on the tip of my tongue, for I am in agony in the flames.'

Abraham replied 'My son, when you were alive you enjoyed all the good things, and Lazarus lived a miserable existence. Now he is being comforted and it is your turn to suffer.

'What's more, there is such a great gulf between us that nobody from our side can cross into yours, and nobody from your side can cross into ours.'

'In that case,' said the rich man's spirit, 'I beg you to send Lazarus to my father's house, for I have five brothers, and he could warn them so that they won't have to come to this place of torture.'

'They have Moses and the Prophets,' said Abraham, 'they can listen to them.'

'Oh, no, father Abraham,' said the rich man, 'but if only someone were to return to them from the dead, then they would have to listen.'

'If they will not listen to Moses or the Prophets,' said Abraham, 'Then even someone rising from the dead will not convince them.' "

THE PARABLE OF THE UNFORGIVING DEBTOR

ST. MATTHEW 18—21-35
ST. LUKE 17—4

Simon Peter asked Jesus, "Lord, how often must I forgive my brother if he behaves badly towards me— as often as seven times?"

Jesus answered, "Not seven times, but seventy-seven. If he does something wrong reprove him and if he is sorry forgive him. And if he wrongs you seven times a day and seven times says 'I'm sorry' you must forgive him."

Then Jesus told the parable of the unforgiving debtor. "A king," he said "decided to square up his accounts with his servants, and began calling in all the people who owed him money.

They brought him a man who owed him millions of pounds, but had no means of repaying the debt. Hearing this the king declared that the man, his wife, and children must be sold into slavery, and all his possessions confiscated, and the money used to pay off some of the debt.

The man threw himself at the king's feet, pleading to be given another chance and time to earn some money towards repayment. The king felt so sorry for him that he cancelled the debt and the man went free.

He hadn't gone far when he met a fellow servant who in turn owed him a few shillings. He grabbed him by the neck and began to shake him, 'Pay me what you owe me,' he demanded. The servant fell at his feet, imploring, 'Please give me time and I will pay you,' but the other refused, and had the debtor thrown into prison.

When his fellow servants found out about this they were very upset, and went to the king and told him the whole story. The king sent for the servant. 'You wicked man,' he said, 'I cancelled the debt you owed to me. Surely you were therefore obliged to show the same pity to your fellow servant.'

And, angrily, he handed him over to the prison authorities until he could repay the debt.

The kingdom of heaven can be compared to that king. And that is how my heavenly Father shall deal with you unless you can sincerely forgive each other."

JESUS SPEAKS OF HUMILITY

ST. LUKE 18—9-14

Jesus talked about false pride. He said "Two men went to the temple to pray. One was a Pharisee, the other a tax-collector.

The Pharisee stood there and said this prayer to himself, 'I thank you God that I am not grasping, unjust, adulterous like other people, and particularly that I am not like this tax-collector here. I fast twice a week, and give money to the Temple, a percentage of all I get.'

The tax-collector stood a little distance away, hardly daring to look up to heaven. And beating his breast to show his sorrow said, 'God please be merciful to me, a sinner.'

The tax-collector went home on good terms with God. The Pharisee did not. For the man who is humble will be raised up. And the man who sets himself above others will be humbled."

132

JESUS AND LITTLE CHILDREN

ST. MATTHEW 19—13-15
ST. MARK 10—13-16
ST. LUKE 18—15-17

People even brought babies and small children to Jesus so that he could touch them. The disciples frowned on this and tried to turn the people away, but when Jesus saw what they were doing he was indignant and said to them, "Don't turn the children away. The kingdom of heaven belongs to little children like these. I tell you solemnly that the people who do not welcome the kingdom of God like a little child will never enter it."

And he put his hands on the children and blessed them.

MARY AND MARTHA

ST. LUKE 10—38-42

Jesus came to a village and was welcomed into the home of two women, sisters called Mary and Martha. Martha was immediately very busy preparing food for their guest, whilst Mary sat herself down at Jesus's feet and hung on his every word.

Martha resented this and said to Jesus, "Can't you see that Mary is leaving me to do all the work. Can't you tell her to help me?"

And Jesus replied, "Martha, my dear, you have chosen to go to a lot of fuss and bother preparing so many things to eat, yet few dishes are needed . . . in fact one simple thing would do. Mary, on the other hand, has made her choice—she has chosen the best part in fact and you must not interfere with her."

THE WOMAN AT THE WELL

ST. JOHN 4—1-42

Jesus was passing through a Samaritan town called Sychar, and, feeling tired, sat down by Jacob's well to rest. It was mid-day, and very hot; he was alone because his disciples had gone into the town to buy food. A Samaritan woman came to the well to draw water and Jesus said to her, "Would you give me a drink of water, please."

Jews did not associate with Samaritans, so the woman, not surprisingly, replied, "What, you a Jew and you ask me, a Samaritan, for a drink?"

"If you knew what God can give," replied Jesus, "and if you knew who it is who is asking for a drink of water, I think you would be asking him for living water."

The woman said, "This well is deep and you have nothing to draw water with. Where can you get this living water? And are you a greater man than our ancestor Jacob who gave us this well?"

Jesus said to her, "Whoever drinks this water will be thirsty again. But whoever drinks the water I give will never be thirsty again. The water I give shall become a spring inside him, welling up into eternal life."

The woman, still not understanding, said, "Sir, please give me this special water so that I may stop being thirsty then I won't have to come to this well to draw water any more."

"Go and fetch your husband," said Jesus, and the woman replied, "I haven't got a husband."

"You're right," said Jesus. "For although you have had five husbands the one you have now is not your husband at all."

"Sir," said the woman, astonished, "I can see that you are a prophet. Our ancestors worshipped on this hillside . . . but you Jews say that Jerusalem is the place to worship . . . "

Jesus interrupted her. "Believe me," he said, "the time will come when worshipping will not be a question of on this hillside or in Jerusalem. You are worshipping with your eyes closed . . . the Jews have their eyes open for the salvation of mankind will come from our race."

"Oh, yes, I understand that the Messiah is coming," said the woman. "And when he comes he will explain everything to us."

"I who am speaking to you," said Jesus, "I am the one."

Just then, Jesus's disciples returned, somewhat surprised to find him deep in conversation with the woman, and she in turn hurried away back to the town

(in such haste that she forgot her water pot) to tell everybody, "Come quickly to see this man who has told me things about myself and my past life. Can this be the Christ?"

Soon a crowd of people began streaming out of the town towards Jesus, many of them already believing in Jesus because the woman had said to them "He told me everything I've ever done." They begged him to stay and talk to them and he stayed for two days, and when he left they told the woman, "We don't believe now just because of what you said, but because we have now heard him with our own ears and we know that this must be the man who will save the world."

JESUS WARNS HIS DISCIPLES OF WHAT LIES AHEAD

ST. MATTHEW 16—13-28
ST. MARK 8—27-39, 9—1
ST. LUKE 9—18-27

One day when Jesus was praying with his disciples, he asked them, "Who do people say I am?"

They answered him that some people said he was John the Baptist, others Elijah, others Jeremiah or one of the prophets.

"But you," he said, "who do you say I am?"

And Simon Peter replied, "You are Christ the Son of God."

"You are a lucky man," said Jesus, "for my Father in heaven has revealed this to you. Now I tell you that you are Peter (which means rock) and on this rock I will build my Church, and it will withstand the powers of death. I will give you the keys to the kingdom of heaven. Whatever you forbid on earth will be what is forbidden in heaven and whatever you allow on earth will be what is allowed in heaven."

He gave them strict instructions not to tell anyone that he was Christ. Then he began to explain to them that he was destined to go to Jerusalem and to suffer terribly at the hands of the elders of the Temple, the chief priests and the scribes, and even to be put to death. But that he would rise on the third day.

Drawing Jesus to one side, Simon Peter started to remonstrate with him. "Heaven preserve you, Lord," he said, "this must not happen to you."

But Jesus rebuked him. "Get behind me, Satan," he said. "Peter you stand in my way when you see things from a man's point of view and not God's."

Then, addressing all the disciples, he said "If anyone wants to be a follower of mine, let him give up his life as it is and take up his cross and follow me. For the man who wants to save his life will lose it and the man who loses his life for my sake will find it.

"What good is it for a man to win the whole world if he ruins his life in the process? For if there are those who are ashamed of me and my words, then I will be ashamed of them when I come with the glory of my Father and his angels to reward each one according to his behaviour on earth."

144

CHAPTER SEVEN

THE TRANSFIGURATION

ST. MATTHEW 17—1-13
ST. MARK 9—2-13
ST. LUKE 9—28-36

About a week later Jesus took Simon Peter, James and John up a high mountain to be alone to pray. As Jesus was praying suddenly he was transfigured, his face shone with an extraordinary brilliance and his clothes became as white as the light. Simon Peter and his companions who had been dozing off woke up abruptly when they saw this and as they watched Moses and Elijah appeared on either side of Jesus, talking with him.

At a loss for words, Simon Peter said, "Lord, it is wonderful for us to be here. Would you like me to make three tents, one for you, one for Moses and one for Elijah?"

But hardly were the words out of his mouth when a bright cloud passed over the sun and plunged them all in shadow, and a voice from behind the cloud said, "This is my beloved son. Pay attention to his words."

The disciples fell on their faces, overcome with fear, but Jesus touched them. "Do not be afraid," he said. And when they looked up he was alone.

As they walked down the mountain he told them to tell nobody what they had seen until after he, the Son of Man, had risen from the dead. They promised, and kept their promise although they discussed among themselves what Jesus could possibly mean by "rising from the dead."

Then they asked him, "What do the scribes mean when they say that Elijah must come first?"

And he answered, "Elijah has come already and they did not recognise him but treated him as they pleased. And the Son of Man will suffer in a similar way at their hands."

And they assumed that he was telling them that John the Baptist had been Elijah.

HIS SECOND WARNING

ST. MATTHEW 17—22-23
ST. MARK 9—30-32
ST. LUKE 9—44-45

Shortly afterwards, when more and more people were coming to admire Jesus and his work, he reminded his disciples, "For your part you must bear this fact firmly in your mind, that the Son of Man will be put to death at the hands of man, and three days after his death he will rise again."

They did not really grasp what he was saying and were embarrassed to ask him. But a great sadness came over them.

150

JESUS ANSWERS: WHO IS GREATEST

ST. MATTHEW 18—1-4
ST. MARK 9—33-40
ST. LUKE 9—46-49

One day the disciples were arguing amongst themselves about which of them was the greatest. Jesus knew their thoughts, so he took a little child and sat it beside him, and putting his arm around its shoulders said, "If anyone wants to be the greatest he must make himself servant of all. Anyone who welcomes a little child like this in my name, welcomes me. And anyone who welcomes me, welcomes the one who sent me."

Then John said, "Master we saw a stranger, healing people in your name. Because he was not one of us we tried to stop him."

And Jesus said, "Don't stop him. A man who works miracles in my name is not likely to speak evil of me. Anyone who is not against us, is for us."

JESUS IS STONED

Jesus was in the Temple at Jerusalem for the festival commemorating the rebuilding of that Temple many years before, and the Jews gathered around him and demanded, "Once and for all tell us plainly if you are the Christ."

But Jesus replied, "You know of, and have seen, the things I do in the name of God. Yet still you do not believe."

The Jews fetched stones to throw at him. Jesus asked them, "Which of all the things I have done in the name of my Father are you stoning for?"

"We're not stoning you for any of the things you have done," they replied, "but for blaspheming. You are a man, and yet you claim to be God."

They were determined to arrest him and stone him to death, but Jesus escaped from them, and went to the far side of Jordan where John had preached and performed many baptisms.

LAZARUS RAISED FROM THE DEAD

ST. JOHN 11—1-44

In the village of Bethany there lived a man called Lazarus who had two sisters, Mary and Martha. Jesus knew them well and loved them very much. One day they sent him a message, "Lord, the man you love is very ill."

Jesus stayed where he was for two more days, before saying to the disciples, "We'll go to Judea."

The disciples thought this unwise for not long before the Jews had tried to stone Jesus to death, and they were worried at the thought of Jesus returning to a place where his enemies wanted to harm him. Jesus said, "Our friend Lazarus is resting, I am going to wake him."

The disciples replied, "If he is resting then surely he will recover."

But Jesus spoke more plainly. "Lazarus is dead. But let us go to him."

So they went. By the time they arrived Lazarus had been dead for four days and was in a tomb. Bethany is not far away from Jerusalem and many Jews from Jerusalem were visiting the sisters to offer their condolences.

Martha hurried out of the house to meet Jesus, and said, "If you had been here my brother would not have died. But I know that whatever you ask of God, he will give it to you."

Jesus said, "Your brother will rise again, Martha . . . "

Martha went into the house and called Mary to see Jesus. Mary got up quickly and went to him, and the Jews who were in the house followed her thinking that she was going to visit the tomb of Lazarus.

As soon as Mary saw Jesus she threw herself at his feet and said "Lord, if you had been here, my brother would not have died."

Seeing her tears, and those of the Jews who followed her, Jesus was very sad and asked, "Where have you put Lazarus?"

"Come and see," they replied and Jesus, weeping, followed them. The tomb was a cave with a stone to close the opening.

"Take the stone away," said Jesus.

Martha said, "Lord, this is the fourth day. By now the body will smell."

But Jesus insisted and they removed the stone from the door of the cave.

Then Jesus prayed to God, and called out in a loud voice, "Lazarus come out."

And the dead man, his hands and feet bound, his face covered with a cloth, came out.

And Jesus said, "Unbind him and let him go free."

HOSTILITY BUILDS UP

ST. JOHN 11—45-54

After this, many of the Jews who had witnessed this miracle believed in Jesus, but some reported back to the Pharisees. So the chief priests and Pharisees called a meeting.

"If we let this man carry on in this way everybody will believe in him and the Romans will come and destroy us all. Here he is working all these signs and we're doing nothing about it."

The High Priest that year was a man called Caiaphas, and he said, "It's better for one man to die than for the whole nation to be destroyed."

And from that moment they were determined to kill Jesus, so that he no longer went about openly among the Jews but left the district and went to live in a place on the edge of the desert called Ephraim, where he stayed with his disciples.

THE BEGINNING OF THE LAST JOURNEY

ST. LUKE 9—51-56

The time for Jesus to be taken up to heaven was drawing near and he set out on the road to Jerusalem, sending some of his disciples on ahead. They went into a Samaritan village to make preparations for Jesus to rest there, but the Samaritans, who knew this was a Jewish pilgrimage to Jerusalem, refused to let him into the village.

James and John wanted to punish the Samaritans for their lack of hospitality. "Let's call down a fire from heaven to burn them up," they said.

But Jesus scolded them for their spitefulness, and they went to another village.

160

CHAPTER EIGHT

HIS THIRD WARNING

ST. MATTHEW 20—17-19
ST. MARK 10—32-34
ST. LUKE 18—31-34

As they journeyed to Jerusalem, Jesus told them for a third time what to expect at the end of their journey. They were walking along the hot, dusty road, Jesus striding ahead of them, and he said: "When we arrive, the Son of Man will be handed over to the chief priests and scribes. They will order him to be put to death. They will hand him over to the non-believers to be mocked and spat upon, whipped until his skin breaks, and crucified. And on the third day he will rise again."

And although they listened, they had no idea what he was talking about.

THE REQUEST

ST. MATTHEW 20—20-28
ST. MARK 10—35-45

James and John, sons of Zebedee, came with their mother to Jesus. "We have a request," they said.

"What is it?" said Jesus.

And they asked for a promise that James and John might sit one at Jesus's left hand, and the other at his right hand in Jesus's kingdom.

"Can you suffer what I am going to suffer?" asked Jesus.

James and John replied, "We can."

"Very well," said Jesus, "then you shall suffer as I shall. But as for promising you certain seats in heaven,
164

these are not mine to give. They belong to those who have already been given them by my Father.''

When the others heard what James and John had asked for they were indignant about it. Jesus called them all around and he explained: "You know that in the heathen world, the rulers lord it over everybody else, and have absolute power. But that mustn't be the case among you. No, if you want to be great, you must be prepared to be a servant. The Son of Man has not come to be served, but to serve others. In fact to give his life for them.''

THE MAN IN THE TREE

ST. LUKE 19—1-10

Jesus had to pass through Jericho on his way to Jerusalem. Among the crowd thronging the route to catch a glimpse of Jesus was a man called Zachaeus, a wealthy man who was one of the senior tax-collectors.

He was anxious to see Jesus but was too short to see above the heads of the others, so he ran on ahead and climbed a sycamore tree which Jesus would have to pass.

As Jesus reached the place where the sycamore tree was, he stopped and looking up said, "Zacchaeus, hurry up and come down because I want to stay at your house today."

Zacchaeus climbed down as swiftly as he could and welcomed Jesus, joyfully. When the bystanders saw the turn of events they grumbled between themselves. "He has gone to stay at a sinner's house," they said.

But Zacchaeus said, "Look sir, I am going to give half of what I have to the poor, and if I have swindled anybody then I am going to repay him four times over."

And Jesus said, "Today this house has been saved, because this man is a son of Abraham, and it was the lost that the Son of Man came to find, and to save."

BLIND BARTIMAEUS

ST. MATTHEW 20—29-34
ST. MARK 10—46-52
ST. LUKE 18—35-43

As Jesus was leaving Jericho with his disciples and a large crowd of followers, a blind beggar called Bartimaeus was sitting at the roadside.

Hearing that Jesus was passing by, he began shouting "Jesus, son of David, have pity on me."

Many people in the crowd told him to be quiet but the more they scolded the louder he shouted until eventually Jesus heard him and stopped.

"Call him over here," he said. So they told the blind man "It's all right now, he's calling you."

Throwing off his cloak, he stood up and went to Jesus.

"Well," said Jesus, "what do you want me to do for you?"

"Master," said the blind man, "let me see again."

Jesus replied, "Go, your faith has saved you."

And immediately the blind beggar was no longer blind, and, seeing, he followed Jesus along the road to Jerusalem

ENTRY INTO JERUSALEM

ST. MATTHEW 21—1-11
ST. MARK 11—1-10
ST. LUKE 19—28-38

They were now drawing very near to Jerusalem and were in fact within sight of Bethphage and Bethany on the Mount of Olives. Jesus sent two of his disciples on ahead and told them, "Go to that village and you will immediately find a donkey and a colt which has never been ridden, tethered in the street. Untie them and bring them here. If anyone asks you what you are doing, reply that the Master needs them and will send them back later."

The disciples did as he told them and sure enough found the donkey and the colt tethered just as he had described. Just as they were untying them, some men standing nearby asked "What are you doing?"

"The Master needs them and will send them back directly," they replied, and the men did not interfere.

They took the donkey and the colt to Jesus and laid their cloaks on the backs of the animals, and Jesus mounted the colt.

As he rode into Jerusalem crowds lined the street and many people threw down their cloaks for him to ride over, and others who had been working in the fields cut great branches from the trees and spread this greenery onto the path before him.

There was tremendous excitement. People were running on ahead, cheering and shouting. "Hosanna," they cried. "God save the Son of David. Blessings on the king who comes in the name of the Lord."

Down the slope of the Mount of Olives he rode and entered Jerusalem and the whole city was in turmoil. Those who didn't know him were asking the others "Who is this?" and the reply came, "This is the prophet Jesus, from Nazareth in Galilee."

JESUS IS MOVED TO TEARS

ST. LUKE 19—41-44

At the sight of the city of Jerusalem, Jesus wept bitterly. "If you only know what is necessary for your peace," he said, "but you cannot see it. The time is coming when your enemies will surround you and conquer you, destroy your buildings and kill your children and all because you did not recognise your opportunity when God offered it."

172

THE PHARISEES COMPLAIN

ST. LUKE 19—38-40

Meanwhile Jesus's disciples were still cheering loudly and happily and some Pharisees in the crowd said to Jesus, "Master, restrain your disciples."

But he replied, "I tell you if *they* kept quiet then the very stones in the road would shout out."

JESUS UPSETS THE TABLES OF THE TEMPLE TRADERS

ST. MATTHEW 21—12-17
ST. MARK 11—15-19
ST. LUKE 19—45-46

He went straight away to the Temple where he was greeted by the usual scene of people buying and selling.

"According to the scripture," he said, "My house will be called a house of prayer, but you are turning it into a robber's den." And with that he upset the tables of the money changers and turned over the chairs of those who were selling sacrificial animals.

There were some blind and lame people in the Temple, and they came to him and he cured them.

"Hosanna," shouted the children in the Temple. And all this was observed by the chief priests and the scribes and they were afraid of him because of the influence he had over the people, and they tried to find a way of getting rid of him.

JESUS AT BETHANY

And Jesus stayed there all day then in the evening left and spent the night at Bethany, at the house of Lazarus, the man whom he had raised from the dead. They gave a dinner in his honour, Lazarus, now completely recovered, sitting at the table and Martha serving the food.

Mary brought out a pound of very costly ointment, prepared from the sweet-smelling plant called Spike-nard. She rubbed it into Jesus's tired feet, wiping them with her hair, until the room was heady with the scent of the ointment.

Judas Iscariot (the traitor amongst Jesus's disciples) said, "Why wasn't this ointment sold—it's worth at least thirty pounds—and the money used to help the poor?"

(Not that he was particularly fond of the poor, but because he was in charge of the funds Jesus collected and was in the habit of putting some of them in his own pocket).

But Jesus replied, "Leave her alone. Let her keep this for my funeral. The poor will always be here . . . but I will not."

Many Jews came to the house, not only to see Jesus but also to see Lazarus, because they knew he had been raised from the dead. The chief priests who had already made up their minds to kill Jesus, decided that they might as well kill Lazarus as well because he was the cause of many Jews going over to join Jesus.

THE WITHERED FIG TREE

ST. MATTHEW 21—18-22
ST. MARK 11—12-14, 20-25

Returning to Jerusalem early the following morning, Jesus felt hungry and seeing a fig tree growing nearby went to it, only to find that it had leaves but no fruit.

"May you never bear fruit again," he said, and immediately the fig tree withered before their eyes. The disciples were amazed at this and expressed their astonishment.

But Jesus reminded them, "If you have faith, and do not doubt your faith, then not only would you be able to do what I have done to this fig tree, but you would be able to tell a mountain to throw itself into the sea and it would do so. Have faith, and everything you ask for in your prayers will be given to you."

178

CHAPTER NINE

THE CONFRONTATION

ST. MATTHEW 21—23-27
ST. MARK 11—27-33
ST. LUKE 19—47-48, 20 —1-8

He went straight away to the Temple and very soon
a crowd gathered around him and he began teaching
them. The chief priests and the scribes, backed by some
other leading citizens had already discussed how they
could get rid of him but their plans were thwarted by the
fact that he had such a huge following amongst the
population.

On this occasion they decided to confront him and
asked him point blank, "What authority have you for
acting like this? Who gave you permission to behave
the way you do?"

"First answer one question," replied Jesus, "and
then I will tell you what you want to know. And this is
my question. John's baptism . . . did it come from
heaven, or from man?"

They argued among themselves what answer they
should give him. After all, if they said that John's
baptism came from heaven, then Jesus would surely
ask, "In that case why did you refuse to believe him?"
And if they said John's baptism came from man, then
they would risk offending the many people who
believed that John was a prophet.

Instead they replied, "We do not know the answer."

"And I," said Jesus, "will not tell you my authority
for behaving as I do."

PARABLE OF THE WEDDING GUESTS

ST. MATTHEW 22—1-14
ST. LUKE 14—15-24

Jesus began to speak to them in parables again. He told them, "The kingdom of heaven could be compared to a king who gave a great feast for his son's wedding. He sent his servants to fetch the guests but they would not come. So he sent some more servants to remind the guests that he had everything ready for the feast. But still they weren't interested, preferring to go about their own businesses, or attend to their farms. Some even attacked the servants who had brought the invitation, and killed them.

When the king heard about this he was furious. Summoning his army, he despatched many troops to seek out the murderers, kill them and set fire to their town.

Then he said to his servants, 'The wedding is ready, but as the guests we'd hoped to have turned out to be not good enough, go instead to the crossroads and invite everyone you see to the wedding.'

So the servants did as they were told and collected an assortment of all sorts of people, good and bad, and the wedding hall was filled with guests.

Then the king came in to receive the guests and noticed one man who was most unsuitably dressed for a party.

'How did you get in, my friend,' he asked the man, 'without being properly dressed for a wedding?'

The man did not reply. Then the king said to the ushers, 'Tie him up and throw him out into the darkness. There he can weep and regret his foolishness.'

For many are invited, but few are chosen."

182

PARABLE OF THE WICKED SERVANTS

ST. MATTHEW 21—33-46
ST. MARK 12—1-12
ST. LUKE 20—9-19

He told them another story. "There was a man who owned land, and planted a vineyard. He fenced it, dug a winepress in it and built a tower. Then he let it to farm-workers and went abroad for a long time. When the time came he sent a servant to collect his share of the vine money from the farm-workers but they attacked the servant and sent him away empty-handed.

The man sent another servant, this time the farm-workers thrashed him brutally. Then he sent yet another servant and this one they killed, and so they dealt with everyone he sent, wounding some, killing others. Until eventually the man decided to send his only son. 'They will surely respect my son,' he thought.

But when the farm-workers saw that it was the son who had come to collect his father's share, they said to each other, 'This is the heir. Let's kill him and take over his inheritance.'

And they murdered him and threw his body out of the vineyard."

Then Jesus asked the people who were listening intently to his every word, "When the owner of the vineyard comes himself, what will he do to those wicked farm-workers?"

They answered him, "He will kill the scoundrels, and lease the vineyard to other tenants who will behave properly and give him his share of the proceeds at the right time."

And Jesus said, "This is the reason that the kingdom of God is to be taken away from you and given to people who will produce its fruit properly."

The chief priests and the scribes knew that this parable was aimed at them and they wanted to arrest him but dared not because they were afraid to upset the crowds who regarded Jesus as a leader.

THE TRICK QUESTION

ST. MATTHEW 22—15-22
ST. MARK 12—13-17
ST. LUKE 20—20-26

Instead, the Pharisees went away and hatched up a plot between them which they thought would trap Jesus. They sent their disciples with some of Herod's supporters who asked Jesus, "Master, we know that you are an honest man and that you are not influenced by other people's opinions or approval. Now tell us . . . is it right to pay taxes to Caesar or not?"

But Jesus, seeing through their deceit, said, "Why try to trap me like this, you hypocrites." Then he said, "Let me see the money you pay taxes with."

So they handed him a silver coin, called a denarius. "Whose head is this?" asked Jesus, "what is his name?"

"Why, Caesar's," they replied.

"In that case," said Jesus, "give back to Caesar what belongs to Caesar, and give to God what belongs to God."

This reply was not at all what they'd expected. They could find no fault with what he said, so they went away.

HE ANSWERS THE SADUCEES

ST. MATTHEW 22—23-33
ST. MARK 12—18-27
ST. LUKE 20—27-40

Then some Saducees (who do not believe in life after death) put this question to Jesus.

They said, "We are taught that if a man dies before he has become a father, then his brother must marry the widow. We know of a case involving seven brothers. The first married and died without children. His brother married the widow, then died before having any children. Then the third brother married her and so on and so on until all seven brothers had been married to the same woman. Then after they had all died, the woman herself died. With life after death, whose wife would she be, having belonged to all of them?"

And Jesus told them, "Children of this world take husbands and wives, but if they are considered to deserve a place in heaven then they are like angels. There's no marriage in the other world."

187

HE ANSWERS THE PHARISEES

ST. MATTHEW 22—34-40
ST. MARK 12—28-34

This remark silenced the Saducees, so then the Pharisees asked him a question.

"Master," they said, "which is the most important of all the commandments?"

And Jesus replied, "The most important commandment is that you shall love the Lord your God with all your heart, with all your soul and with all your mind. And after that the next most important commandment is to love your neighbour as you love yourself."

FALSE SCRIBES

ST. MATTHEW 23—1-10
ST. MARK 12—38-40
ST. LUKE 20—45-47

While all the people were still listening intently he changed the subject and said to his disciples, "Be on your guard against the scribes who like walking around in flowing robes, and having people bow to them in public, take the front seats at the synagogue and the best places at dinner parties. They profit from the property of widows and cover up for themselves with lengthy prayers. These men are heading for severe punishment."

THE WIDOW'S MITE

ST. MARK 12—41-44
ST. LUKE 21—1-4

All this time people were coming in, putting their offerings into the collecting box. Some rich people put in a great deal but Jesus noticed a poor widow drop in two small coins, worth about a penny, and he said, "I tell you truly that this poor widow has put in more than any of the others. For they have given what they could easily afford to give, but she has given everything she has."

THE END OF THE TEMPLE

ST. MATTHEW 24—1-44
ST. MARK 13—1-37
ST. LUKE 21—5-36

As he was leaving the Temple, one of his disciples drew Jesus's attention to the building itself. "Look at the size of these stones, Master. How enormous they are."

And Jesus replied, "You see these great buildings? Not a single stone will remain, everything will be destroyed."

"When will this happen," they asked him. "What will be the sign that the end of the world is coming?"

And Jesus told them, "The sun will be darkened. The moon will lose its brightness. The stars will fall out of the sky and the heavens will shake. And the Son of Man will appear in the clouds, strong and glorious and he will send his angels to every corner of the earth to fetch the ones he has chosen to be with him in heaven.

"Be on your guard and stay awake, for if he comes unexpectedly he mustn't find you asleep.

193

THE PARABLE OF THE BRIDESMAIDS

ST. MATTHEW 25—1-13

"The kingdom of heaven will be like this: like the ten bridesmaids who took their lamps and went out to meet the bridegroom. Five of the bridesmaids very sensibly took their lamps and also took flasks of oil. But five bridesmaids were foolish and took their lamps but no extra oil. The bridegroom was a long time coming and they all felt very drowsy and fell asleep. Suddenly, in the middle of the night there was a shout 'Here comes the bridegroom'. They all got up and the five foolish bridesmaids said, 'Oh, dear, our lamps are going out,' and they asked the five sensible bridesmaids for some oil. But the sensible ones realised they would need all their oil themselves.

So the foolish bridesmaids hurried off to the shop to buy some oil, and whilst they were away the bridegroom arrived. Those bridesmaids who were ready went in with him to the wedding party, but the others returned to find the doors closed and could not get in.

And that's why I tell you to be on the alert."

194

JESUS DESCRIBES THE
DAY OF JUDGEMENT

ST. MATTHEW 25—31-46

Then Jesus told them how it would be on the day of Judgement. He said, "When the Son of Man comes, in his splendour and with all his angels around him, he will sit on his glorious throne. All the people will be collected in front of him, and he will separate them as a shepherd separates sheep from goats.

He will place the sheep on his right-hand side, the goats on his left-hand side. Then he will say to those on his right, 'Come you who have earned my Father's blessing. This kingdom has been kept for you since the beginning of time. For I was hungry and you gave me food. I was thirsty and you gave me a drink. I was lonely and you gave me friendship. I was naked and you gave me clothes. I was ill and you cared for me. I was in prison and you came to see me there.'

Then these honest people will say to him, 'Lord, when did all this happen?' And the king will answer, 'I assure you that by doing this for the least important of my brothers, you did it for me.'

Then, turning to those on his left-hand side he will say 'Go away from me, you who have been cursed, go into the fire which is blazing for the Devil and his angels! For I was starving and you gave me nothing to eat. I was thirsty and you gave me nothing to drink. I was a stranger and you never welcomed me. I was naked and you gave me no clothes. I was sick and in prison and you never visited me.'

And they, in their turn will ask, 'But Lord when did we see *you* like this?' And he will reply, 'I assure you that by neglecting to help the humblest of my brothers, you neglected to do it for me.'

And they will suffer punishment for ever. And the good will enjoy life for ever."

JESUS WAITS

ST. LUKE 21—37-38

As the feast of the Passover drew near, Jesus waited, spending his nights on the hill called Mount of Olives, and his days in the Temple, talking to the people who gathered eagerly around him.

198

CHAPTER TEN

THE END DRAWS NEAR

Two days before the feast, and having finished all his teaching, Jesus called his disciples around him and told them, "As you know it will be Passover in two days time, and the Son of Man is going to be betrayed, and crucified."

THE PLOTTERS

ST. MATTHEW 26—3-5
ST. MARK 14—1-2
ST. LUKE 22—1-2

Meanwhile the chief priests and senior citizens were discussing a way of getting rid of Jesus. They met in the palace of the High Priest, whose name was Caiaphas, and planned how to have Jesus arrested by some trick and then killed. And they agreed on one thing, "It must not happen during the festivities for that could cause a riot amongst the people."

202

THE BETRAYER

ST. MATTHEW 26—14-16
ST. MARK 14—10-11
ST. LUKE 22—3-6

Then Judas Iscariot, one of the disciples, went to the Temple police with a plan for handing Jesus over to them. They were delighted. "What will you give me in return?" he asked, and they handed over thirty pieces of silver on the spot. From that moment Judas Iscariot waited for the right time to betray Jesus, without the people knowing about it.

PLANS FOR THE PASSOVER

ST. MATTHEW 26—17-19
ST. MARK 14—12-16
ST LUKE 22—7-13

When the time of the Passover feast came, the disciples asked Jesus, "Where do you want us to eat the Passover supper?"

And he said to Simon Peter and John, "Listen, as you go into the city you will see a man carrying a jug of water. Follow him and he will go into a house. Go into the house and say to the owner 'The Master says where is the room in which I can eat Passover with my disciples?' He will take you upstairs to a large room furnished with couches, and prepared for the supper. Make arrangements for us to eat there."

They set off and found everything just as he had said it would be, and prepared the Passover.

204

THE LAST SUPPER

ST. MATTHEW 26—20-23
ST. LUKE 22—14-23
ST. MARK 14—17-25
ST. JOHN 13—1-21

The time came for supper, and Jesus sat down at the table with his disciples. "I have waited to eat this meal with you," he said, "for now it is time for me to suffer and believe me I shall not eat the Passover again until all that it really means is fulfilled in the kingdom of God."

Then Jesus got up from the table, took off his robe and tied a towel around his waist. Then he poured water into a basin and kneeling began to wash his disciples' feet, and to wipe them with the towel.

When he came to Simon Peter, the disciple asked, "Surely you aren't going to wash my feet?" And Jesus answered, "At the moment you do not quite understand what I am doing. Later you will."

When he had finished, he put his clothes on again and went back to his place at the table and said, "Do you understand what I have done? You call me teacher and Lord which is right for I am. If I as Lord and teacher can wash your feet, this is an example to you, and you must be ready to do the same for each other."

Then he took some bread and, after saying grace, broke the bread into pieces and gave a piece to each at the table, and said, "This is my body, take it. Do this in memory of me."

Then taking a cup of wine he passed it to each of them saying, "This is my blood which will be poured for you. I tell you truly that I shall drink no more wine until the day I drink the new wine with you in the kingdom of heaven."

And then he said, "There is someone sitting at this table who is going to betray me." They were all very distressed at this. "Not I, Lord," they said, each in turn including Judas Iscariot.

JESUS PREDICTS THE BETRAYAL

ST. JOHN 13—21-30

Jesus repeated, "I assure you one of you will betray me."

The disciples looked at each other, wondering whom he could possibly mean. John, the disciple Jesus loved most of all, was reclining on the couch beside him and Simon Peter said to John, "Ask him which of us he means."

And John, leaning towards Jesus, asked "Who is it, Lord?"

And Jesus said, "It is the one to whom I shall now give this piece of bread," and with that he handed a piece of bread to Judas Iscariot. Then Jesus said to Judas Iscariot, "What you are going to do, do it quickly."

None of the others knew what he meant. They thought that as Judas looked after their funds, Jesus was telling him to go out and buy something or else to give something to the poor.

As soon as Judas had taken the bread, he got up from the table and went outside into the night.

208

THE DISCIPLES' PROMISE

ST. MATTHEW 26—30-35
ST. MARK 14—26-31
ST. LUKE 22—31-34
ST. JOHN 13—36-38

They sang psalms then left the house, walking to the Mount of Olives. On the way there Jesus told them, "Before the night is over, you will lose faith in me." Turning to Simon Peter he said, "I have prayed for you so that your faith may not fail, and once you have recovered you in turn must strengthen your brothers."

Simon Peter said, "Even if all lose faith in you, I would not. I would be ready to go to prison with you. I will lay down my life for you."

"Lay down your life for me?" answered Jesus, "I tell you before the cock crows today you will have denied three times that you know me."

"If I have to die with you I will never disown you," said Simon Peter and all the disciples said the same.

JESUS TALKS OF GOD

ST. JOHN 14—1-10

Then Jesus said, "Don't be upset. Trust God and trust me. My father's house has many rooms and I am going to get a place ready for you, and I shall return and take you with me so that we can be together. You know where I am going, and you know the road I am going to take."

Thomas said, "Lord, we don't know where you are going so how can we know the road you are going to take?"

Jesus replied, "I, myself, am that road, and the truth, and the life. No one approaches the Father except through me."

Philip said, "Lord, let us see the Father and then we shall be satisfied."

"Have I been with you all this time," said Jesus, "without your really knowing me? If you've seen me, you have seen the Father."

JESUS PRAYS ALONE

ST. MATTHEW 26—36-46
ST. MARK 14—32-42
ST. LUKE 22—39-46

They came to a vine-grove called Gethsemane on the Mount of Olives. "Pray that you won't have to be put to the test," he told them. Then he walked a short distance away, leaving the disciples except for Simon Peter, and the sons of Zebedee who went with him. He seemed overwhelmed with sadness. "My heart is almost breaking," he said. "Wait here and keep awake with me." Then he went on a little farther alone and, kneeling on the ground, prayed.

213

He came back to the disciples and found them sleeping.

"Can't you keep awake with me for one hour?" he asked. A second time he went away and prayed, and came back to find that again they had fallen asleep. Leaving them, he went away and prayed for a third time.

He returned and said to them, "Now you can sleep. It is all over. The time has come for the Son of Man to be betrayed into the hands of evil men. Look, here comes my betrayer."

THE ARREST

ST. MATTHEW 26—47-56
ST. MARK 14—43-52
ST. LUKE 22—47-53
ST. JOHN 18—1-11

At that moment they were surrounded by Roman soldiers and Temple police, armed with torches and weapons and carrying lanterns. At their head was Judas Iscariot, who knew where to find Jesus because the garden was a favourite place of his. Judas had already arranged with the soldiers to identify Jesus by kissing him.

"Greetings, teacher," he said and kissed Jesus.

"Judas," said Jesus, "are you betraying the Son of Man with a kiss? My friend get on with it and do what you came for."

Then he stepped forward. "Who are you looking for?" he asked the soldiers.

"Jesus of Nazareth," they said.

He said, "I am Jesus." They took a step back, and again he asked them "Who are you looking for?"

"Jesus," they replied.

"I have told you, I am he," said Jesus. "I am the one you are looking for. Let these others go."

As the soldiers went to seize Jesus his disciples said "Lord, shall we use our swords?" Simon Peter drew his sword and wounded the high priest's servant, Malchus, cutting off his right ear. Jesus said, "Put your sword back." And touching the man's ear, healed it.

Then, speaking to the soldiers, he said, "Am I a criminal that you had to come for me armed with swords and clubs. I have been sitting among you in the Temple for days and you never attempted to lay hands on me then."

Then they seized Jesus and his disciples turned and ran away. The soldiers grabbed at one of them, who was wearing a loose linen robe, catching hold of the cloth but he slipped out of it and escaped, naked.

TRIAL AT NIGHT

ST. MATTHEW 26—57-68
ST. MARK 14—53-65
ST. LUKE 23—63-71
ST. JOHN 18—12-28

The Roman soldiers and the Jewish guards bound Jesus and took him to Caiaphas the High Priest where the scribes and elders were gathered together. Simon Peter followed at a distance and when the crowd reached the priest's palace, Simon Peter went in and sat with the servants to see what would be the outcome.

The priests and the Sanhedrin (which was the Jewish court of law) were looking for evidence, even if it was false evidence, which would give them an excuse to condemn Jesus to death.

Several lying witnesses came forward but their evidence wasn't strong enough. Then two men stepped forward and said that Jesus had told them he had the power to destroy the Temple and rebuild it in three days.

The High Priest then asked Jesus, "Do you have anything to say to that?"

Jesus was silent.

Caiaphas said, "Tell us if you are Christ, the Son of God."

"I am," said Jesus.

At this the High Priest cried, "Blasphemy. We do not need any further witnesses. You've all heard the blasphemy . . . what is your verdict?"

And everybody shouted, "He deserves to die."

They blindfolded him and spat in his face and hit him. "Who was that who hit you, Christ?" they mocked. "Prophesy that!"

SIMON PETER'S DENIAL

ST. MATTHEW 26—69-75
ST. MARK 15—66-72
ST. LUKE 23—54-62
ST. JOHN 18—12-28

Whilst Jesus was being questioned, Simon Peter was sitting outside in the courtyard, warming himself by the fire. A servant girl saw him, "You, too, were with Jesus," she said.

"I don't know what you're talking about," said Simon Peter. He moved away from the fire and presently another servant approached him, a relative of the man whose ear Simon Peter had cut off. "You too were with Jesus the Nazarene," he said.

"I don't even know the man," said Simon Peter.

Then some bystanders said, "You are one of them for sure, your accent gives you away."

Then Simon Peter began cursing them and shouting "I don't know the man."

At that moment there was the sound of a cock crowing and Simon Peter remembered that Jesus had told him, "Before the cock crows you will deny me three times."

Then Simon Peter went outside, and broke down and sobbed bitterly.

SENTENCED TO DEATH

ST. MATTHEW 27—1-26
ST. MARK 15—1-20
ST. LUKE 23—1-25
ST. JOHN 18—28-40, 19—1-16

Dawn came and all the Jewish assembly marched with Jesus to Pontius Pilate (the Roman Governor) to make their complaints against him.

"This man has been corrupting the people, telling them it is wrong to pay taxes to Caesar, claiming that he is Christ, a king," they said.

Pilate turned to Jesus, "Are you the King of the Jews?" he asked.

"Yes, I am a king," said Jesus. But my kingdom is not in this world. If it were, my men could have fought for me."

"I can't find anything *criminal* about this man," said Pilate to the chief priests and the crowd.

But they weren't satisfied and insisted . . . "He is a troublemaker with his teachings all the way through Judea from Galilee to this place."

Hearing this Pilate realised that as a Galilean Jesus came under Herod's rule, and as Herod happened to be in Jerusalem at that time, Pilate passed Jesus over to Herod.

Herod was pleased to see Jesus because he had heard a lot about him and had been hoping to see him with his own eyes. He was also hoping that he might see Jesus perform some miracle, so while the chief priests and scribes gathered outside he questioned him at length but Jesus did not reply to his questions.

Herod and his guards made fun of Jesus, even to the extent of putting a rich ceremonial cloak on him, and then they sent him back to Pilate.

Pilate called the chief priests and the leading men and the people and said, "You brought this man to me, telling me he was a troublemaker, and I've gone into the matter and I can find no proof against him. Neither can Herod, for he has sent him back to us.

"Since the man has done nothing to deserve death, I'll have him whipped, then set him free."

It was the custom to release a prisoner at Passover time so this would have been quite in order. But the crowd shrieked, "No. Set free Barabbas." (This was a man who was in prison for murder and causing a riot).

Pilate realised that it was out of jealousy that the priests and scribes were against Jesus. Also during the day his wife had sent him a message warning him to have nothing to do with the death of Jesus. "I have been upset by a dream I had about him," she said. Pilate didn't want to get too involved with the affair.

"What am I to do with this man who is King of the Jews?" he asked, and they screamed with one voice: "CRUCIFY HIM. CRUCIFY HIM."

Pilate could see that the crowd was in a dangerous state. He called for some water, and in front of the crowd washed his hands saying "I am innocent of this man's blood. It's your affair."

Then he ordered Barabbas to be set free, and he ordered Jesus to be whipped, then handed over for crucifixion.

223

JUDAS' REMORSE

ST. MATTHEW 27—3-10

When Judas heard that Jesus had been condemned to death, he was overcome with remorse and went back to the chief priest and the elders taking the thirty pieces of silver.

"I have done wrong," he said, "I have betrayed an innocent man."

"That's your business," they said. "It's no concern of ours."

He threw down the money, went out and hanged himself. The chief priests picked up the money but agreed that they couldn't put it back into the Temple funds because it was blood-money, so they used it to buy a field as a burial place for foreigners.

CHAPTER ELEVEN

MOCKERY

ST. MATTHEW 27—27-31
ST. MARK 15—16-20

The soldiers took Jesus to the inner part of the palace called the Praetorium. They dressed him in a fine purple robe and twisted some thorns into a crown and put that on his head. They put a reed into his hand, and making fun of him knelt saying, "Hail, King of the Jews." Then they took the reed out of his hand and hit him on the head with it. Finally they took off the fine purple robe, dressed him in his own clothes and led him away to be crucified.

THE CRUCIFIXION

ST. MATTHEW 27—32-56
ST. MARK 15—21-41
ST. LUKE 23—26-49
ST. JOHN 19—17-37

The place for the crucifixion was called Golgotha (which means place of skulls) and on the way there they came across a traveller called Simon from Cyrene, and asked him to help carry Jesus's cross. There were two others to be crucified with Jesus that day, one on either side of him. Pilate wrote out a notice and had it fixed to Jesus's cross. It said: Jesus the Nazarene, King of the Jews.

The writing was in Hebrew, Latin and Greek. The Jewish chief priests objected to the words. "You shouldn't write: King of the Jews, but: This man said, 'I am King of the Jews'" they said.

But Pilate answered, "It's written and that's that." They offered Jesus wine mixed with myrrh which he tasted but refused to drink.

When the soldiers had finished nailing Jesus to the cross they divided his clothing into four shares, one for each of them. His undergarment was in one piece, and since they didn't want to tear it they threw dice to see who should have it.

"Father, forgive them, they do not know what they are doing," said Jesus.

The crowd jeered at him. "You said you could rebuild the Temple in three days, how about saving yourself and come down from the cross," they shouted.

"He saved others yet he cannot save himself," said the priests and scribes.

"If you're the Son of God, let God rescue you," cried others.

One of the criminals, hanging beside him, said, "If you're Christ, save yourself and us as well."

But the other spoke up. "We deserved our sentence," he said, "Jesus has done nothing to deserve it. Jesus, will you remember me when you come into your kingdom?"

"I promise you," Jesus replied, "that today you will be with me in paradise."

Then the sun was covered, and it was very dark and this lasted for three hours. Near the cross stood Jesus's mother, and his mother's sister Mary the wife of Clopas, and Mary Magdalene. Seeing his mother and the disciple, John, whom he loved standing near to her, Jesus said to his mother "Woman, this is your son." And to the disciple he said, "This is your mother."

Then those standing near to the cross heard him cry, "My God, my God, why have you deserted me?"

Somebody ran and soaked a sponge in rough wine and putting it on the end of a reed stretched it out and held it to his mouth.

After he had drunk it, Jesus said, "It is accomplished." His head fell forward and he died.

At this precise moment the veil of the Temple was torn in two, and there was an earthquake. The Roman soldier who was guarding Jesus said: "Truly, this was the Son of God."

In accordance with the custom, the soldiers came to break the legs of the men who had been crucified. They broke the legs of one man, then the other, but when they came to Jesus they saw that he was dead, and so instead of breaking his legs one of the soldiers pierced his side with a sword and immediately there came out blood and water.

Many of his friends stood at a distance, including the women who had come with him from Galilee, and they saw all this happen.

THE BURIAL

ST. MATTHEW 27—57-61
ST. MARK 16—42-47
ST. LUKE 23—50-56
ST. JOHN 19—38-42

Then a member of the Jewish council who had secretly been a disciple of Jesus arrived. His name was Joseph and he came from Arimathaea, a Jewish town. He had not agreed with what the others had done to Jesus and now he went to Pilate and asked for the body of Jesus. Pilate, astonished that Jesus should have died so quickly, sent for the soldiers to ask if he was already dead. When they assured him that Jesus was dead, Pilate told Joseph he could take the body, and Joseph then took the body down off the cross. He wrapped it in a clean linen cloth with spices, following the Jewish burial custom and laid Jesus in a tomb which had been cut out of the rock.

Then Joseph put a huge stone at the opening of the tomb, and went away as it was the beginning of the Sabbath.

The women who had been with Jesus, watched where Joseph put the body then they went away and prepared spices and ointments.

234

THE GUARD

ST. MATTHEW 27—62-66

The following day the chief priests and Pharisees went to Pilate because they were worried that Jesus had said, "After three days I shall rise again." They were afraid that his disciples might steal the body and then tell the people that Jesus had indeed risen from the dead. They wanted permission to place a guard near the tomb to make sure that this did not happen.

Pilate said, "You may have your guard." So they went and made sure that the entrance to the tomb was secure, and left several Temple soldiers guarding it.

CHAPTER TWELVE

THE RESURRECTION

ST. MATTHEW 28—1-10
ST. MARK 16—1-8
ST. LUKE 24 –1-9
ST. JOHN 20—1-18

On the morning of the following day, it was still quite dark, and Mary Magdalene went to the tomb. She saw that the stone had been moved away from the tomb, and ran back to Simon Peter and John.

"They have taken Jesus, and I don't know where he is," she said. Both disciples hurried to the tomb. They saw the linen clothes lying on the ground, and Simon Peter went right into the tomb and saw the cloth that had been over Jesus's head. They understood then that Jesus had risen from the dead. They went home. But Mary remained there, weeping. After a while, she stooped to look inside and saw two angels dressed in white. They were sitting where the body of Jesus had been, one at the head and one at the feet.

"Why are you crying?" they asked her.

"Because they have taken my Lord away and I don't know where they have put him," she said. As she said this she turned and saw another man standing there. It was Jesus, but she did not at first recognise him.

"Why are you weeping? Who are you looking for?" he asked her.

Mary thought he must be the gardener. "Sir, if you have taken him away, please tell me where he is."

Jesus said, simply, "Mary." And then she knew him.

"Master," she said, overjoyed.

Jesus said to her, "Do not cling to me. I have not yet ascended to my Father. But go and find the brothers, and tell them that I am soon to go up to my Father, your Father. My God who is your God. And tell my brothers they must leave for Galilee. I will see them there."

Mary did as Jesus told her.

The women told their story, but at the time it seemed pure nonsense and very difficult to believe.

THE STRANGER ON THE ROAD TO EMMAUS

ST. MARK 16—12-13
ST. LUKE 24—13-35

That same day two of the disciples were on the way to a village called Emmaus some miles outside Jerusalem. Of course they could talk of nothing but the events of the past few days. As they were walking, engrossed in their conversation a man joined them. They thought it was a stranger but in fact it was Jesus and they didn't recognise him.

"What are you talking about?" he asked them. They stopped at once, their faces sorrowful.

The one called Cleopas answered, "You must be the only person for miles around who doesn't know what's been going on in Jerusalem the last few days," he said.

"Oh, what's that?" asked Jesus.

"Why, all the things concerning Jesus of Nazareth," said Cleopas, still not recognising that it was Jesus he was talking to. "Jesus the one who was a great leader. We had all hoped that he would be the one to lead Israel to freedom, but our chief priests and scribes had him crucified. The crucifixion happened two whole days ago, and now we are all astonished by some women from our group who went to the tomb to find him gone. And they say that the angels told them he is still alive. Some of our friends also looked into the tomb, and he was gone."

"What foolish men you are," said Jesus, and began to explain to them all the passages from the scriptures which referred to Jesus. They were still talking when they arrived at the village, and the two disciples insisted that Jesus should spend the evening with them, and he agreed.

They sat down to supper together, and Jesus took the bread and broke it and handed them each a piece. With this simple act they suddenly realised who he was, and at that moment of recognition he disappeared.

Immediately they hurried back to Jerusalem to report to the others, only to hear that meanwhile Jesus had appeared to Simon Peter.

243

JESUS RETURNS

ST. MARK 16—14-15
ST. LUKE 24—36-43
ST. JOHN 20—19-23

They were still talking about all this, in a room with locked doors for they were afraid of the Jews, when Jesus appeared standing with them. Alarmed and frightened they thought they were seeing a ghost.

"Peace be with you," said Jesus. "Why are you so worried. Look at the marks on my hands and feet . . . . you can see it is I. Touch me if you wish . . . I am flesh and bones, nothing ghostlike at all."

Then they were so overjoyed that they were speechless.

245

THOMAS IS CONVINCED

ST. JOHN 20—24-29

Thomas, one of the disciples was not with them when all this happened, and later when the others told him about it he was disbelieving.

"Unless I can see with my own eyes the holes where the nails went into his hands and feet, and touch with my own hand the hole in his side where they pierced him, then I refuse to believe what you say," said Thomas.

Eight days later the disciples were again together in the house, and this time Thomas was with them. The doors were closed, but suddenly Jesus stood among them.

"Peace be with you," he said. Then, turning to Thomas, he said, "Look, here are my hands," and he showed him the marks of the nails. Then taking Thomas's hand he said, "Look, here is the hole in my side. Put your hand there and feel for yourself.

"Don't have any more doubts. Believe what you see."

Thomas, knowing that this was indeed Jesus, said, "Teacher, my God."

And Jesus said, "Yes, now you believe because you can see me. It's even better to be one of those who has not seen yet can still believe."

247

THE STRANGER ON THE BEACH

ST. JOHN 21—1-14

Some days later the disciples were fishing by Lake Tiberias. They had been fishing all night without having caught a thing. As it grew light, they were aware of a man standing on the shore, but they didn't know who it was.

"Have you had a good catch, friend?" called out the man. "No," they replied.

"Cast the net again, and you'll find something," said the man. So they dropped the net, which was immediately so heavy with fish that they couldn't haul it in.

"It is the Lord," said John, realising that the man was in fact Jesus.

' At this they all started scrambling about to get the boat and fish into land, and as they came ashore they saw that there was a small meal prepared of bread, and fish cooking over a charcoal fire.

"Come and have breakfast," said Jesus, "and bring some of the fish you have just caught."

They dragged the net ashore marvelling that although it was full of big fish it was not broken. Jesus shared the bread and the fish he'd cooked among them.

None of the disciples was bold enough to ask, "Who are you." But they knew without asking that it was Jesus.

248

THE ASCENSION

ST. MATTHEW 28—16-20
ST. MARK 16—15-20
ST. LUKE 24—50-53

Jesus visited them once more. They were together in a room and he led them as far as the outskirts of Bethany, to a high place, and he blessed them all. And then he told them, "Go out into the world and tell the good news to everyone. Find new followers in every country and teach them what I have taught you, and know that I shall be with you always, to the end of time." And after this he walked a few paces away and stood by himself, and, standing there, was carried up to heaven.

His disciples watched, then, full of happiness and hope they turned and took the road back to Jerusalem.

THE ACTS
OF THE
APOSTLES

THE BEGINNING OF THE CHURCH IN JERUSALEM

ACTS 2

It was the day of Pentecost, a harvest festival, and Jesus's apostles, who were in the habit of meeting daily were in a room together. Peter and John, James and Andrew, Philip and Thomas, Bartholomew and Matthew, James son of Alphaeus and Simon the Zealot, and Jude son of James, and also Matthias who had been selected to take the place of Judas Iscariot.

Suddenly the entire house was filled with the sound of rushing wind, and tongues of fire licked into the room, and, separating came to rest on the head of each man. Immediately they began speaking to each other in foreign languages, and understanding each other.

In Jerusalem at that time were many religious men from other countries and they quickly gathered at the house and to their astonishment each heard his own language being spoken. Parthians, Medes, Mesopotamians, Elamites, Asians, Egyptians, Libians, Romans, Cretans, men from Judaea, Cappadocia, Pontus and Phrygia and Pamphylia . . . all listened in amazement to these men whom they knew to be Galileans speaking in other tongues. They could find no explanation for this.

A few tried to laugh it off. "They're drunk," they declared, but Peter corrected them. "Hardly drunk," he said, "at nine o'clock in the morning."

Then Peter talked to the people about Jesus and his crucifixion and as they listened they were deeply touched. Throughout the day more than three thousand people came forward to be baptised.

These were the first Christians. They set up their own community, sold their possessions and shared the money between themselves providing for each according to his needs. They went to the Temple every day to pray, and met in each other's houses to break bread as Jesus had done at the last supper.

People admired them for their kindness and generosity, and the miracles worked through the apostles aroused great interest, so that each day more people joined them.

254

CURE OF THE LAME BEGGAR

ACTS 3—1-10

There was a forty-year-old man who had been crippled from birth, who spent his days sitting begging at the Beautiful Gate near the Temple. One day as Peter and John were on their way to the Temple they passed this beggar who was being carried by his relatives. Seeing them he held out his hand to beg for something, but Peter said "I have no money but I will give you what I have. In the name of Jesus, walk." And he took the beggar's hand and helped him to stand up. As he did so the cripple's feet and ankles became strong and he began to walk and jump about. Then still clinging to Peter and John he went with them to the Temple recognised by everybody as the beggar who used to sit at the Beautiful Gate, and the people talked among themselves but could find no possible explanation for this miraculous cure.

THE DECEPTION OF ANANIAS AND SAPPHIRA

ACTS 4—32-35
ACTS 5—1-11

The apostles were frequently in trouble with priests at the Temple for continually talking of Christ's resurrection. At the same time their fame spread, attracting more people to join them. Although they had no possessions, they were never in need, for people gave them money, often selling their land or houses in order to raise money to give.

There was a man called Ananias who agreed to sell some property and give the money to the apostles. But having sold it he couldn't quite bring himself to part with all the money so he and his wife Sapphira agreed to keep some of it back and pretend it had fetched a smaller price.

When he gave the money to the apostles, Peter said: "The land was yours. When you had sold it the money was yours. Why should you lie? You have lied to God." At this Ananias fell dead to the ground.

The people watching were shocked and some of the younger men carried the body away to be buried. Some hours later Sapphira came in, unaware of what had happened. Peter challenged her: "Was this the price you got for your land?" he asked. "Yes" she replied.

"So you thought you could trick God," said Peter. "What made you do such a thing?" The sound of footsteps could be heard outside.

"Do you hear that?" said Peter "they have been to bury your husband, they will bury you too."

At that Sapphira fell dead at his feet and the young men took her and buried her beside her husband.

THE DEAD WOMAN RAISED TO LIFE

ACTS 9—36-43

The apostles worked many miracles. One day one of the disciples, a woman called Tabitha (sometimes known as Dorcas) of Jaffa was taken ill and died. She was a very good woman, who spent her days caring for others, and the disciples who lived with her washed her body and laid it in an upstairs room. Then, having heard that Peter was in the neighbouring town of Lydda, they sent for him.

He came at once and went to the room where the body of Tabitha lay, surrounded by her friends and women weeping, showing him the beautiful needlework Tabitha had sewn when she was alive. Peter sent them out of the room, then knelt by the body and prayed. After this he looked straight at the body and said "Get up, Tabitha."

And she opened her eyes and sat up, and he gave her his hand and helped her to her feet. Then he called the disciples and showed them that Tabitha was alive again.

STEPHEN IS STONED TO DEATH

ACTS 6—8-15
ACTS 7—1-60
ACTS 8—1-3

Stephen, one of the apostles, began to work many miracles and when people from the synagogue came forward to argue with him they found they couldn't fault his wisdom. So they bribed some men to say that they had heard Stephen using blasphemous language. Then they had him arrested and brought before the Sanhedrin.

Stephen tried to persuade the members of the council that what he said and did in the name of Jesus was right, but everything he said made them more angry.

Suddenly Stephen looked up into the sky and saw God with Jesus standing on his right.

"I can see Heaven wide open," he told the council, "with Jesus standing at God's right hand."

This enraged the members of the council. They blocked their ears with their hands and shouted at him, then they dragged him outside the city wall and stoned him.

It was hot and some of them took off their clothes and put them at the feet of a young man called Paul (sometimes known as Saul) so that he could mind them. Paul watched the death of Stephen, entirely approving of the stoning.

That was the beginning of a bitter persecution against the Christians and many of them had to run away for their safety to the country districts of Judaea and Samaria where they spread the teachings of Jesus. Meanwhile Paul was working to destroy the Church in Jerusalem and went from house to house looking for Christians whom he arrested and sent to prison.

PAUL'S CONVERSION

He was so intent on killing Jesus's disciples that he even asked the high priest to give him a letter of introduction to the synagogues in Damascus, authorising him to arrest any Christians, men or women, he could find there and fetch them back to Jerusalem.

On the road to Damascus just outside the city, he was suddenly halted by a brilliant light all around him. It was such a shock that he fell to the ground and then he heard a voice say: "Saul, Saul why are you persecuting me?"

"Who are you, Lord?" asked Paul, and the voice replied "I am Jesus, and you are persecuting me. Get up, and go to Damascus and there you will be told what you must do."

The men travelling with him were speechless for although they had seen the dazzling brilliance and heard the voice they could see no one. The light went, and Paul groped his way to his feet, for even with his eyes wide open, he could see nothing.

His companions led him by the hand into Damascus. Meanwhile a disciple called Ananias who lived in Damascus had a vision in which Jesus told him to go to Paul. "You will find him in the house of Judas in Straight Street, Damascus," said Jesus. "He is Saul of Tarsus, he is praying, having had a vision of a man called Ananias coming in and laying hands on him to restore his sight."

At this Ananias replied: "Lord, I've heard of this man, and I know all about the harm he has been doing to your disciples in Jerusalem. I know too that he has come here with a warrant to arrest everybody who acts in your name."

"Nevertheless I have chosen him to work for me," replied the Lord. "You must go and do as I say."

So Ananias went to the house and found Paul there, and touched him, saying "Brother Saul, I have come from Jesus to restore your sight, so that you will be filled with the Holy Spirit."

And at once it was as if scales had fallen from his eyes and Paul could see again. They baptised him, and then he was given food, for he had not eaten for three days.

ESCAPE IN A BASKET

ACTS 9—20-30

He stayed with the disciples in Damascus for a few days and then began at once preaching in the synagogues and telling the people that Jesus was the son of God. Those who heard him were amazed, for it was common knowledge that he was the man who had come from Jerusalem expressly to arrest Christians.

The Jews at Damascus were quite confused by this and also by the things he said, and after a time they worked out a plot to kill him, keeping watch on the city gates so that he could not escape.

But the disciples found out about the plot and when it was dark they put Paul in a basket and lowered him from the top of the wall. He returned to Jerusalem, to join the disciples there. At first they were wary of him, remembering his past record, but Barnabas intervened, telling them about Paul's vision on the road to Damascus, and of the work he had done in Damascus. After this he began working with the disciples, until they found out about a plot to kill him, and they sent him away to Tarsus for safety.

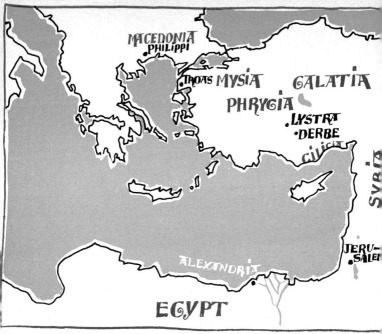

PAUL'S TRAVELS

ACTS 15—36-41
ACTS 16—1-10

One day whilst they were praying Paul and Barnabas were told by God that he wanted them to set off on the work for which he had called them and they went to preach the story of Jesus, in foreign lands. They travelled far, but later they quarrelled and split-up, then Paul chose Silas to be his companion, and continued his missionary work.

They travelled through Syria and Cilicia, Derbe and Lystra, strengthening the faith of the churches and establishing new ones. They passed through Phrygia and Galatia, having been instructed not to preach there, through Mysia and Troas.

One night Paul had a vision in which a man said: "Come to Macedonia to help us." He lost no time in arranging to go to Macedonia, convinced that this was a message from God.

262

IMPRISONMENT AND DELIVERANCE

ACTS 16—11-40

They stayed at Philippi, one of the main cities in Macedonia, and one day as they were going to pray they met a slave girl who told people's fortunes. Immediately she tagged on to them shouting "These men are God's servants. They have come to show us how to be saved."

Each day she repeated this until eventually Paul became irritated and turning, said "I order you to leave that woman," and the evil spirit left her and she was quiet. Her masters, who profited by her fortune telling now had no further chance of making money out of her and they were very angry. They seized Paul and Silas and dragged them to the market place, before the magistrates.

They charged Paul and Silas "These men are causing a disturbance." The crowd shouted agreement, and the magistrates ordered Paul and Silas to be stripped of their clothes and whipped, then they were thrown into prison.

The gaoler, who had been warned to keep a close watch on them, put them into the innermost cell, with their feet secured in stocks.

Night came, and as Paul and Silas were praying and singing hymns, there was a sudden earthquake that shook the very foundations of the prison. The doors flew open, the prisoners' chains fell from them.

The gaoler, wakened by the noise, saw the doors open and drew his sword to kill himself, sooner than await punishment for letting his prisoners escape. But Paul shouted to him. "Don't harm yourself, we are all here."

The gaoler rushed in with lights to see for himself, and realising that they must be men of God was very frightened.

"What must I do to be saved?" he asked them and they told him "Become a believer in the Lord Jesus and you will be saved and so will all your family."

Then he washed their wounds and he and all his family were baptised, then they sat down to a celebration meal together.

The next morning the magistrates, afraid that there could be some connection between the earthquake and the men they had imprisoned, sent word to the prison to release Paul and Silas. The gaoler gave this news to Paul, but Paul refused to leave.

"Do they think they can treat Roman citizens this way, throwing us into prison without a trial, then sending us on our way!" he declared.

When the magistrates heard this they were appalled to learn that the men they had imprisoned were Roman citizens for they had believed them to be Jews. Immediately they hurried to the prison and begged Paul and Silas to leave.

So they did, and continued on their travels.

264

PAUL THE CAPTIVE

ACTS 21—27-40
ACTS 22, 23, 24, 25, 26, 27, 28

Paul was in the Temple in Jerusalem when some Jews who were against him started shouting "This is the man who has been going around preaching against us." People came running and the mob, whipped up into a frenzy, dragged Paul out of the Temple beating him. He was within inches of his life, but soldiers at a Roman garrison nearby heard the pandemonium and men were sent at once to quell the riot.

Paul was arrested and put in chains. It was impossible to question him on the spot because of the noise of the crowd, so the soldiers carried him to the fort. They were under the impression that they had captured an Egyptian who was wanted for having organised a revolt, but when Paul spoke to them in Greek they realised their mistake.

He asked permission to talk to the crowd and standing at the top of the stairs he spoke to them in Hebrew. He told them of his earlier life when he persecuted the Christians, of the men and women he had sent chained to prison and death. He told them what had happened to him on the road to Damascus, of his blindness and how his sight had been restored.

All the while they listened to him. Then Paul added that once when he was praying in the Temple at Jerusalem God appeared to him and told him to leave Jerusalem for the people there would not believe him, and go instead to preach to the pagans in far-away lands.

At this the crowd burst out afresh, yelling and throwing things. This brought the soldiers running and the tribune (the man in charge) ordered him to be whipped, for he thought Paul was concealing something and that this would make him speak the truth.

When they had strapped him down, Paul turned to the soldier on duty and asked "Are you legally entitled to flog a Roman citizen without a trial?"

This stopped the soldier in his tracks. He went to the tribune and told him what Paul had said. Then the tribune himself came to Paul to ask him if this was true, and when he realised that he had chained a Roman citizen he was worried.

The following day he ordered a meeting of the chief priests for he wanted to know what were their charges against Paul, then he had Paul brought before them. But the meeting became completely disorganised with the Jews fighting between themselves, and the soldiers took Paul back to the fortress for his own safety.

That night the Lord appeared to Paul and told him "Have courage. You have testified for me in Jerusalem. Now you must do the same in Rome!"

In the morning the Jews met and hatched a plot to kill Paul. They planned to ask for Paul to be brought for another meeting and they would lie in wait for him and kill him. They vowed not to eat or drink until they had accomplished this. But Paul's nephew, the son of his sister, heard of the ambush and went to the fort with his story.

The tribune did not want any harm to come to
the prisoner in his charge, so he arranged for Paul to be
escorted to the governor of Judaea, a man called Felix,
and to ensure his safety he provided four hundred
soldiers and seventy cavalry.

They left at night and delivered Paul to the governor
at Antipatris. The governor read the letter written
by the tribune, and arranged for the Jews to bring
their case against Paul to him. He listened to their
arguments but when Paul mentioned the coming
judgement, Felix was afraid and told the Jews he
would adjourn the case for the time being. He kept
Paul prisoner for two years, often sending for him
to talk to him about his beliefs

Felix was replaced as governor by Festus who was immediately asked by the Jews to bring Paul to trial. He had Paul brought to him, and Paul protested his innocence. Festus was keen to remain on good terms with the Jews so he suggested that Paul should go to Jerusalem for trial.

But Paul insisted. "I have done the Jews no wrong, if I am to be tried it must be before the court of Caesar." And Festus was compelled to agree. A few days later King Agrippa and Bernice his sister arrived and Festus told them all about Paul.

"I should be interested to meet him," said Agrippa, so the following day Paul was brought before the assembled company and Agrippa invited Paul to tell his story.

When Paul had finished Agrippa was very impressed. "You have almost convinced me of becoming a Christian like you," said Agrippa.

"I wish not only you but everybody else here today would be like me . . . except for these chains," replied Paul.

Then Agrippa and Bernice and Festus talked together and agreed that Paul had done nothing to deserve death or imprisonment, but reluctant to free him without authority they decided to send him to Rome.

Paul, and some other prisoners in the charge of a Roman Centurion called Julius, put to sea. After a few days they ran into a fierce storm, so severe that the captain had to throw the cargo overboard, and then the ship's gear. For several days the storm raged and it seemed as if they could not survive, but Paul told them, "Don't despair. God has told me that I shall appear before Caesar. We will lose the ship but not our lives. We are to be stranded on an island."

Just before daybreak on the fifteenth day, Paul said "Fourteen days you have been worried and not eating. Your safety is not in doubt, eat now," and with this he took some bread, broke it and ate it, thanking God.

When it was light they saw they were close to an island. The vessel ran aground and began to break up. Some of the soldiers planned to kill the prisoners to prevent them escaping but the centurion in charge would not let them. Some swam ashore, others floated on pieces of wreckage. All landed safely.

The island was called Malta. They stayed there for three months then went on to Rome where Paul taught and preached freely.

THE BOOK OF REVELATION

JOHN'S VISION OF THE FUTURE

REVELATION 4—1-5

In my vision I saw a door in heaven open and heard a voice like a trumpet speaking to me. And it said "Come up here. I will show you what is to happen in the future." And I saw a throne in heaven, and the person sitting on the throne looked like a diamond and a ruby. And a rainbow, like an emerald, encircled the throne. Around the throne was a circle of twenty-four thrones, and twenty-four elders sat on these thrones, dressed in white robes with golden crowns on their heads. Dazzling shafts of lightning were coming from the throne and the sound of thunder.

Then I saw a new heaven and a new earth. The first heaven and the first earth had disappeared, so had the sea. And I saw the new Jerusalem coming down from God out of heaven, like a bride dressed for her husband. Then I heard a voice calling from the throne in heaven "Now God will live among the people. He will wipe away their tears. And there will be no more death, no more mourning, nor sadness."

Then an angel took me to the top of a mountain and showed me the new Jerusalem. It glittered like a precious diamond. The walls were vast, with twelve gates, at each gate an angel and over the gates were inscribed the names of the twelve tribes of Israel. The walls of the city stood on twelve foundation stones, each one bearing the name of one of the apostles. The angel carried a gold measuring rod and he measured the city. The walls were built of diamond and the city itself of pure gold, shiny as polished glass. The foundations of the city contained precious stones, diamond, lapis lazuli, turquoise, crystal, agate, ruby, gold quartz, malachite, topaz, emerald, sapphire, amethyst. Each gate was a single pearl. The main street was pure gold, as clear as glass.

There was no temple in the city, because the Lord God and the Lamb were the temple. And the city was lit by the radiance of God, so it did not need the sun and moon for light.

I am John the one who saw and heard these things. And I knelt at the feet of the angel but he told me: "Don't kneel at my feet. I am a servant like you. It is God you must worship."

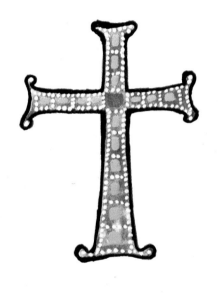

ST. JOHN 21-25

There were many other things that Jesus did; to write them all down would fill more books than the world has room for.